the leap of the deer

the
Leap of
the Deer

---

memories
of a celtic childhood

Herbert O'Driscoll

COWLEY PUBLICATIONS
Cambridge ♦ Boston
Massachusetts

Published in the United States of America by Cowley Publications, a division of the Society of St. John the Evangelist. No portion of this book may be reproduced, stored in or introduced into a retrieval system, or transmitted, in any form or by any means—including photocopying—without the prior written permission of Cowley Publications, except in the case of brief quotations embodied in critical articles and reviews.

Library of Congress Cataloging-in-Publication Data:
  O'Driscoll, Herbert, 1928–
    The leap of the deer: memories of a Celtic childhood/Herbert
      O'Driscoll.
      p. cm.
    ISBN: 1-56101-086-3 (paper)   1-56101-093-6 (cloth)
    1. O'Driscoll, Herbert, 1928–   —Childhood and youth. 2. Church of
  Ireland—Clergy—Biography. 3. Anglican Communion—Clergy—
  Biography. 4. Ireland—Social life and customs—20th century. 5.
  Country life—Ireland. 6. Civilization, Celtic. I. Title.
    BX5595.036A3 1994   283'.092—dc20
    [B]   93-41744

The landscape on the cover is taken from a photograph of the Paps of Anu, County Kerry, Ireland.

This book is printed on recycled, acid-free paper and was produced in the United States of America.

Cowley Publications
28 Temple Place
Boston, Massachusetts 02111

contents

pRelUOe

Summer 1949. In Ireland the ghosts of kings speak in place names. As you drive southwest from Cork City you are driving toward a kingdom, the kingdom of Kerry. The way to this kingdom is through a land that becomes increasingly lonely and rugged as you travel. The coastline, wherever you come to it, at places such as Ballingeary, is rugged and deeply indented from its struggle with a fierce and cold Atlantic. Now and again there are beaches that call the traveler by their beauty, as the sirens once called Ulysses and his crew. Like the sirens, they promise more than they provide. To walk these beaches is to taste the luxury of silence and solitude; to swim from them is to freeze the bones of even the bravest.

Like any kingdom worthy of the name, these borderlands between Cork and Kerry have about them a touch of magic. Having passed through places with names such as Macroom, Rosmore, and Inchageelagh, you see ahead of you the Shehy Mountains. Your way through them is called the Pass of Ceimaneigh.

Ceimaneigh is the attempt of some long-ago English mapmaker to put together the three Gaelic words that in English mean "the leap of the deer." As you move through the pass, you wonder at the thought that any deer could ever have leaped such a distance, but then you remind yourself that here you are not in a kingdom of mere one-dimensional legends. In Gaelic myth and story the deer is not merely an animal. In more than one story Irish saints have taken upon themselves the shape of a deer to avoid danger or to flee from enemies. It is said that thus Patrick and his monks reached Tara and the high king's palace as they went on Easter Eve to challenge the druids and the old pagan deities.

So you look again through your windscreen at the pass and you no longer ask unworthy questions of dull and prosaic fact. If you are wise, you presume that the place is not called Ceimaneigh without good reason. Who knows the truth of that long-ago leap taken in or out of time? Who knows what form the great animal may have had before or after the majestic flight from promontory to promontory? If in the kingdom of Narnia it is possible for the deity to assume the form of a lion, why in this kingdom cannot it be the form of a deer?

I first passed through Ceimaneigh when I was twenty and nearing my twenty-first birthday. A college friend and I drove in an old and laboring Morris car which would eventually take us to Kerry, around Killarney, across the Shannon, through Clare, and into Galway. Of the miles we covered, the jokes we shared, the friends we made, the camping places where we pitched and struck our small tent evening and morning, there is not much to tell, if only because we have all taken such journeys in one way or another.

The reason I mention our journey at all is that, all unknowing, I was about to be shown another and greater kingdom. At that time my friend George had discovered the person of Jesus of Nazareth in a way that made him, for my friend, Christ and Lord. We would sometimes talk of that. We would struggle with the seeming contradiction by which this discovery linked our Lord to a church that seemed to us as youths so dull and uninspiring. In thoughtful moments we would acknowledge that in spite of its dullness this same old church had taught us anything we now knew about Jesus Christ. In the years to come we would resolve these things, each in his own way. Perhaps, as with most Christians, we would never fully resolve them. However, like the young man healed of his blindness by our Lord and introduced to us by John the Evangelist, I can now say of that long-ago summer that I who had been blind received my sight. Like the deer, I made the leap from mere traditional, institutional faith to personal faith. All that followed—university, ordination, ministry in many places—began with that leap.

The world of these pages is that of Ireland in the middle of this century, and within it an even smaller world, that of the Church of Ireland. Even more precisely, these pages are an attempt to describe one particular life in that little world. Above all, it was an island world, long in memory, deeply conservative, imaginative, romantic, artistically creative, gentle and good humored yet also depressive and, on occasion, even brutally violent. In the Republic, as distinct from Northern Ireland, the vast majority of its people were Roman Catholic in religion, a form of Roman Catholicism that may well be the world's most faithful and resilient of that vast communion.

Within this Roman Catholic world there was a smaller but still very influential world. All of us in it were referred to as Protestants, a term that included anybody who was not Roman Catholic. The largest community within this Protestantism was that of the Church of Ireland, the province in Ireland of the Anglican Communion. Ironically, the Church of Ireland has always tended to be wary of the word "Anglican" for much the same reason as the Episcopal Church in the United States. In both cases the word "Anglican," with its overtones of "English," allowed those who wished to condemn it as a foreign and essentially disloyal body to do so. This was true in Ireland from the Reformation on, and in the United States from the years following the War of Independence to the present day.

We Irish Anglicans were hybrid creatures, schizophrenic in our loyalties and in our sense of self-identity. We were not Roman Catholic but we were taught to insist on our claim to be the sons and daughters of the pre-Reformation church in Ireland just as much as those who were Roman Catholic. In a word, we were taught to claim that it was quite possible to be Irish and Catholic without being *Roman* Catholic. As children we were never given the impression that our tradition began with the Reformation. As I look back now, I realize that we tended to see the Reformation as a distant European event. For us, the stories of faith took us back to the early Christian centuries, especially the fifth to the tenth.

However, let us leave such things for later pages. For now, let me say by way of introduction that I am a priest of the Anglican Communion whose ministry has to this point extended across the second half of this century. During those decades the world has radically changed, so much so that the immensity of change threatens to obliterate memory. As Europe reaches further west and embraces the eastern Atlantic, absorbing societies by new worlds of communication—not to mention the great truck trailers that now thunder ceaselessly through village streets once designed for donkey carts and pony traps—the little world of the south of Ireland is being remorselessly changed. Doubtless this future will bring both good and evil, but whatever it brings it will be different from what has been. That is the way of things and always will be.

As these changes come they also erode old ways of believing, old forms of institutional religion. Not only the Church of Ireland, but all forms of institutional faith are being changed, even the most faithful sons and daughters of Rome. Before such change obliterates forever the kind of church and world in which I was a child and in which I was ordained a priest, I wish to outline its face as one would the face of a parent or grandparent seen in a painting that is already fading. To do so is also to pay a debt of gratitude.

father martin

I n good weather, the top half of the front door of the farmhouse is left open so that my aunt or whoever is in the house can look down the driveway to see if anyone is coming. Because I am only six years old, even the half-door is still too high for me to see over. I rush to the small kitchen window, climb a chair, and sweep aside the corner of the white lace curtain.

Suddenly and unforgettably, she enters my world. The woman's skin is darker than I am accustomed to seeing in my pale Irish elders. Her clothes are ablaze with color, and around her head is a kerchief that seems to emphasize her flared cheekbones and dark eyes. In her arms is a baby, and beside her is a boy about my own age, bronzed and barefooted.

"The gypsies are here," says my aunt, her tone wary and tense. She moves to the half-door as if to establish a boundary for the approach of the strangers.

Season by season they would come in those days, rolling along the narrow roads in their brilliantly painted caravans. Choosing a suitable place by the side of the road, the gypsies would settle down for a few days, rest their lean, piebald horses, hang out some washing to dry, and approach the local farms.

Sometimes the men would ask for a little work to earn some money, but they seldom got it because they were deeply mistrusted as thieves of fowl and livestock. The women would approach the house itself.

She came to the door. I watched from my window perch, wondering what it would be like to be able to play with her boy. Somehow I knew instinctively that it would never be allowed, which made my longing even more acute. The woman spoke very softly. She really didn't need to make herself heard because the encounter was so much a part of Irish country life that it required no dialogue. The request would always be for some tea or milk or bread or a few eggs. I watched my aunt turn back into the kitchen, reaching in various shelves and cupboards, placing the rich brown eggs into the woman's hand, from which they would disappear into the deep pocket of her flowered apron. With them went some of the morning's white milk for the baby, poured into a tin can swinging at the woman's side by its thin wire handle. Then, and only then, did the woman smile, her teeth, darkened by tobacco and strong tea, showing for a moment. "May your son be a priest," she said softly and turned away, disappearing around the gate at the end of the driveway.

It was an expression of thanks immediately understood in the Ireland of those days. The greatest joy and privilege for a Roman Catholic family was to have a son in the priesthood or a daughter in one of the women's orders. Furthermore, this attitude permeated the whole of society, so that in the Church of Ireland as well it was considered a joy and privilege if a son "went into the ministry." In this, and indeed in many other subtle ways, the Church of Ireland was very much part of the world that surrounded it.

In that Ireland of the late 1930s, priesthood was at once mundane and mysterious, familiar and exotic, cherished and resented. Its embodiment was everywhere, from brown-robed, jovial friars to earnest, black-suited seminarians. Rarely seen alone, the clergy almost always appeared in pairs or in groups, moving along the sidewalks of the city streets, standing in the endless line-ups for the magical world of the cinema, or cheering their favorite team from the sidelines on a weekend afternoon. They represented the vast contribution of Ireland to world Roman Catholicism. Their rural Irish faces would redden under African and Australian suns, or grow pale in chancery offices in Chicago or Boston.

Consider, for instance, Father Martin. He was the second son of a large family who lived a few farms over from us. Martin grew up with my uncles until one day he left home and we heard he went to the seminary at Maynooth. It was said that Martin was "going into the priesthood"—the very phrase is an image of how the news was received in those days. By going into the priesthood, one was entering into another kind of world, another level of being. Maynooth itself, a vast complex of buildings west of Dublin, was held in awe by ordinary folk. Behind its great doors lay another world, another set of laws, another mode of being, another way of looking at history and at time itself. Not for a moment am I suggesting that there was not comradeship, laughter, relaxation, and much humanity, but there was also the sense of an absolute severance from one's former life.

What happened afterward, where one went after the seminary years and eventual ordination, became a minor question. One had already gone, so it did not matter where. Nairobi, New York, Brisbane, Patagonia—all merged and became one in a kind of sacred geography. After all, it was not for nothing that the word "catholic" was taught to mean universal.

Then word came to the farm that Father Martin was being sent to Australia. In that earlier and sterner church he would not have expected any choice in the matter, nor would he have been given any. The day Martin had lain prone in his new vestments before the altar in the cathedral, eyes closed and forehead touching the marble floor, he had willingly ceased to be a creature of choice. He had made the greatest choice conceivable in his world. Nothing remained but to obey.

When the news came of his departure for Australia, there was a certain sense of loss not only in his family, but also in ours, who were only friends and neighbors, and Protestants at that. For most ordinary folk even today, Australia is a distant place; in those days the very word had a ring of finality. To say goodbye to someone bound for Australia, standing on the cobbled quayside in Dublin, waving a forlorn handkerchief at the ferry heading out into the Irish Sea for Holyhead or Liverpool, might well be a farewell forever. Yet this sense of family loss, communicated to me by a younger brother of Martin's about my own age, had an extraordinary muted quality. It seemed as if the leaving of Father Martin—he would never again, not even by his family, be referred to as

Martin—was only the extension in geography of a severance that had taken place on the day he walked through the gates of Maynooth.

So Father Martin passed from the familiar Kilkenny countryside, as did tens of thousands of his generation. Over the years news of him would come. It would be reported along the little roads that he had had some illness, but, thank God, had recovered. He would appear back on furlough, not staying long around the farm because he would be about the church's mysterious business in important places like Dublin or Maynooth. But when he was at home, Father Martin would greet and be greeted by all in the neighboring farms, Protestant and Catholic alike.

I can recall watching such an encounter as a small boy. It took place in a bend in the road where a small lane branched off into the fields. My uncle was speaking to an elderly neighbor whose front gate he had just fixed. Both were leaning on the gate, myself perched on the top bar, when Father Martin came around a further bend in the road. As soon as he came into view I was aware of a slight tension, a deliberate preparation for this encounter.

Of course the meeting was pleasant and jocular, with greetings offered and acknowledged, but familiarity had somehow become bounded by intangible and undefinable limits. Martin, who as a boy had for years driven the cows morning and evening through this very gate, who had carried his schoolbag down through these same fields, whose swinging stick had sent a leather ball high over these white birch trees, was in some mysterious way the same yet not the same. His person, although not at all changed in its stocky peasant body, was, like the Blessed Sacrament he handled at Mass, now strangely changed—familiar in appearance, changed in substance.

Some years later word came that Father Martin was "having a little trouble with the bottle." The phrase expressed the same Irish taste for euphemism that would describe a time of vicious and bloody civil war as "the troubles." As we know now in a more sophisticated if not wiser world, Martin was not alone in his priestly battle with alcoholism. There was no condemnation of him, merely concern and sadness. Then word came that he had been cured, but neither his fall from grace nor the human vulnerability it pointed to lessened in any way the reality of his priesthood.

Thus we were taught at a very early age the distinction between priesthood and sanctity. Both might indeed sometimes dwell together in one person; there had been and would again be great priests who were also great saints. But the absence of sanctity did not mean the absence of priesthood, nor the loss of one mean the loss of the other. Priesthood was seen as something beyond mere clothing or role or even behavior. It was a reality embodied fully in one's humanity and capable of being betrayed by that same humanity, but never blotted out or destroyed.

the

shoemaker's son

The coast of County Waterford stretches between Wexford to the east and Cork to the west. For the most part, Waterford is a county of gentle rolling countryside. To the north, separating it from Tipperary, is the blue-green line of the Knockmealdown Mountains.

Norse sailors liked to come to this coastline for one reason: the eastern side of the country is deeply pierced by the kind of wide river estuary that was suitable for the quick Norse raid followed by an equally quick departure. By night, and sometimes even by day, the longboats would sweep in from the sea, enter the estuary, and probe further up the narrowing river until they came upon the first monastery or settlement. If they had had sufficient warning, the monks would have gathered the livestock into the fortified enclosure and hidden the church valuables in the nearby high round tower. They themselves would climb the ladder to the lowest entrance—about twenty feet above the ground. Here there would be stocks of water and basic food, sufficient to wait out the Norse invaders, who were never anxious to stay longer than necessary. When the besieged saw the longboats slipping down the river toward the sea, they would come down and life would go on until the next raid. But if there had been no prior warning of the raid, the screams of the dying would be heard for a long distance. Some women and children from the nearby settlement would be carried to the waiting ships, the monastery building would be ransacked, some monks killed or taken prisoner, fires set.

Eventually, as with all things, the Norsemen passed from history. Some of them stayed in these green hillsides and settled among those whom they came to plunder. There is even some evidence that a few became monks, mingling their voices in the cycle of liturgy that rang ceaselessly down through the centuries, and leaving their bones in these pastures. Over time other monasteries rose here, as they did all over Ireland. One of them was called Mount Mellory.

The Trappists of Mount Mellory had built well, prospering through the years by farming the land, adding to their buildings, and attracting many to their stark community life. When the bells of the great tower rang out, the winds off the Atlantic seemed to carry their ringing far beyond normal hearing.

I remember well when I first became aware of Mount Mellory as a small boy living in Cork City in the neighboring county. According to today's concepts of distance Mount Mellory was actually very near to us, not more than fifty miles or so away, but in those days such a distance, especially to a child, was infinitely remote. Yet Mount Mellory reached into my life through the most simple but effective of ways.

The shop of Mr. McCarthy, the shoemaker, stood about a hundred yards from where I lived. It was not a shop in the sense in which we would understand that term today because it was the McCarthys' home. Like many houses in that world of long ago it was small, its front door low and narrow, and when you entered you stepped down onto a concrete or stone floor. Again, as with many houses, there was a half-door over which customers could lean to ask Mr. McCarthy or his son if their shoes were done.

The two of them sat in the middle of the room on two short wooden benches. At the end of each bench was a shiny metal stand shaped at the top like a shoe, and on these stands the work was done. A tiny window let in so little light as to ensure an early loss of vision on the part of anyone trying to work by it. Around the edges of the room were shelves where rows of shoes of every description lay. It now occurs to me to ask to whom these shoes belonged. Were they for sale? Or had they been left by people who had brought them for repair and later leaned many times over the half-door in the forlorn hope of having them returned, but, finally, despairing of success, left them to Mr. McCarthy to do with them what he would?

When I was sent to the shop as a child, I would reach up and over for the latch and call out, to be invited in by a gruff shout. Mr. McCarthy, a stocky, bald man who always wore a black leather apron and a cloth cap no matter what the season of the year, was a formidable figure to a small boy. Yet it was his son, Brendan, who filled me with a sense of fearful curiosity. He, too, was aproned. He was always bent over his work. He never spoke.

In the fashion of those days, all the work was done by hand. Each man would deftly cut the leather, punch the holes, draw the stitches through, and bang in the nails. Neither seemed to communicate with the other at any time. Sometimes while I waited for a pair of shoes I would become aware of a stillness that was oppressive in spite of its being broken by the sounds of the work. If one man needed a tool from the other, an outstretched hand was sufficient request. Yet even a child could sense the son was distant, his movements slow; it seemed as if he were absent although he was physically present. To a child it was puzzling and even frightening. I never heard Brendan utter a word. As I look back now from the perspective of adulthood, I suspect that he was in his early twenties and probably had a mental handicap of some kind. At that time and in that society, there would have been no medical or psychological resources whatsoever to be brought to bear on the situation.

There came a day when I took down a pair of my father's shoes for repair and for the first time I saw that Mr. McCarthy was sitting alone. He was hard at work as usual, but the bench where Brendan had always worked was unoccupied. No tools were beside it. No shoes ready to be repaired lay around it. As a child I did not ask where Brendan was. Neither I nor anyone else saw him again.

Eventually word passed among the neighbors that Brendan had been taken to Mount Mellory. To a child the news had a mysterious and rather frightening quality about it. Brendan's going had been so sudden and so silent that my mind played fearfully with the thought that I myself might also be taken up by unknown hands and spirited away to those imagined great gates that would crash closed behind me forever and ever, where I would never play again, never see my parents again, never be free again.

Life went on. To my knowledge, Mr. McCarthy sat in the tiny darkened room and plied his trade until his hands would no longer obey him. Decades later, to a changed and worldlier Ireland there would come the various therapies and medications that would treat a young life like Brendan's, turned deeply in upon itself. Such lonely journeys of the mind as his would be named, categorized, analyzed, and treated. But in that older society there was as yet no such naming of these things. It had simply been seen that Brendan was not as a youth of his age should be, that the deep shadows in his mind would never lift, and that his parents were growing older and were poor. No clinics and social programs existed to respond to this need, but, in quite another way, resources did exist.

There existed in Mount Mellory and in other large monastic communities a separate world where Brendan could go. In that world there was a community large enough to assimilate and accept him. There he could function within his limitations and take his place in its life, and there his skills would be used. Somewhere in the vast monastery complex Brendan would be given another bench, another set of tools. Once more he would bend and shape the leather for the sandals and workboots of the community.

At Mount Mellory he would have security and identity as a lay brother in the vast society of the monastery. His parents would never again have to worry about his welfare. In fact, they would forever receive the gift of his prayers and enjoy the benediction of having a son within a community of holiness and contemplation. Once or twice in their lifetimes they might take the long journey, alighting from a bus, nervously pulling the bell that rang down the long halls beyond the gates. From such a journey they would return to their little home to pick up once again leather and hammer and worn shoes, remembering with pride the dark, cowled figure whose silence, once sad and frightening, was now transformed for them into a holy silence and thus given dignity and meaning.

Perhaps such a glimpse of family life is the best way to express the relationship of the Roman Catholic Church to society in that pre-World War II Ireland. The church did not lie within society, but was in itself a parallel society. It was not simply one aspect of life, but possessed a vast and powerful life of its own. The church did not see itself as part of society, but rather saw society as a child to be nourished, guided, corrected, and disciplined. If a certain child had needs to which that society could not respond, if the father of that child came one evening, hat literally in hand, and asked a favor of the local parish priest for his son, that request would enter the hidden channels of the church's life and receive consideration by faces and voices unseen and unknown. A decision would be taken, the half-door into the McCarthy's little house would be opened, and Brendan would be gently led from his home to the car waiting to take him to his new life behind the gates of Mount Mellory.

conflicting
loyalties

When people ask me about growing up in the south of Ireland I often hear in their voices and in their questions the unspoken assumption that absolute divisions existed between Catholics and Protestants. When I hear those assumptions, I begin to recall certain faces and voices that come back to remind me that the web of relationships in which I grew up was a much more subtle and complex reality than most people think.

Mrs. Wilson was a tiny, dark-haired woman who came to do housework for my family, and among her duties was looking after me. On most days she and I would leave the house and go for a walk down by the fisheries, that part of the river where the fishing boats came in. I loved that walk because the river broadened just enough to allow quite large, ocean-bound freighters and ferries to go further up to the city docks. I realize now that it was my first contact with the idea of other, faraway worlds.

Mrs. Wilson, whom my parents called Nancy, had the sallow face and drawn features that very often meant tuberculosis in that society. I remember that she smoked incessantly and that she laughed a great deal. Sometimes when she laughed her face would change and pucker up, her body would bend over, and she would be racked by a bout of coughing. Nancy married while she still worked for us, but I cannot recall the actual occasion. She would have been married in the local Roman Catholic chapel and it would have been unthinkable for our family to attend, yet her wedding was the occasion of great joy on our part. We would have given her a gift and I remember that the little reception was held in our parlor. Nancy remains very clearly in my memory, and among her gifts to me was teaching me the Lord's Prayer.

Another memory. Each summer, when we went for a number of weeks to my grandfather's farm in County Kilkenny, I would meet Paddy Byrne again. Paddy lived on a farm further up the side of the valley. He was about two years older than I was, but each summer we would meet again and go around together. Once we investigated the loft of an old ruined cottage, very nearly falling through the rotten floors and ceiling. In later years, when we were about eleven and thirteen, we would trespass on the new golf course on the farm next to his and search for golf balls, and I think it was that same summer when we sat in the shelter of a high ditch and shared a few puffs on a cheap Woodbine cigarette, probably taken from Paddy's father's pocket.

But on Sundays we went our separate ways, he to Mass at Immaculate Conception Church and I to Anglican Morning Prayer at St. Mary's. To my knowledge, we never spoke of these things. I suspect they were such total givens in our lives that they were beyond words. Yet at no time did that gulf come into our friendship. I realize now that our parents were not threatened by such early relationships across the Protestant-Catholic gulf, although that would have come if our friendship had continued into adolescence. Ours was not unlike children's friendships across the gulf of color in the American south.

And three years later I was in boarding school and became aware of Mr. Power—Paddy to his colleagues but certainly not to us. A slim, olive-skinned, dark-haired man, he had a marked sense of the dramatic. When Mr. Power swept into class, his teacher's gown flowing out behind him, his books clasped in the crook of one arm, he was an imposing figure. He spoke and taught English, Gaelic, French, and Spanish. He was the only Roman Catholic member of the staff, probably because it was difficult to find qualified Protestant teachers who could teach the Gaelic language. Mr. Power gave me one of the things I treasure most in my life, a love of English literature and drama. He took us with him into the world of Shakespearean plays and into our own, half-lost Gaelic world, showing us by his own voice and intonations how beautiful its poetry was, how full of earthy humor its prose.

Unlike the other teachers, Mr. Power lived outside the school and we knew that he differed from all of us in that he was Roman Catholic. I never met him in later years, and, leaving the country, I lost track of him. But I remember him as a figure of infinite romance. My memories of him contain something undefinable, exotic, mysterious. A strong Spanish strain runs through Irish culture, brought in the sixteenth

century by the wrecking of many of the ships of the
Spanish Armada on the west coast of Ireland. I often
wonder if Mr. Power embodied that strain, introduc-
ing us to a larger world and implicitly calling us to a
cosmopolitanism our island once possessed but had
long since lost.

In some ways it is true to say that the Church of
Ireland was a ghetto, but reality is never as simple as
it looks when viewed from the outside. The truth is
that the relationship between its people and the surrounding Roman Catholic world was much more
complex. A ghetto suggests walls, area, definition.
There were very few of these things, at least in the
geographical sense, and it would have been very difficult to define any particular part of the city as specifically Protestant or Roman Catholic. Our world
simply did not know the kind of grim realities that
years later would become Northern Ireland, with a
Protestant street and a Catholic street, where danger
would lurk for the trespassing outsider. By virtue of
our being a tiny minority—about ten percent of the
population—most Protestant families were surrounded by Catholic neighbors, and for the most
part that word "neighbors" aptly describes the relationships that existed.

Only in certain circumstances were walls suddenly
erected to bring relationships to an end. If young
people of a Protestant and a Catholic family wanted
to marry there would be much consternation, particularly on the Protestant side over Roman Catholic
inflexibility about the marriage service and the religious upbringing of children. Furthermore, when a
member of a Protestant family became seriously ill,

every effort would be made to enter a hospital that was generally acknowledged—but not specifically defined—as Protestant.

Apart from such eventualities, however, in the ongoing flow of daily life friendships developed, things were borrowed and returned, fields were mutually rented, help was exchanged at harvest time, and children played in each other's homes. As we grew older we would sometimes find ourselves questioning this great divide in our lives, yet since almost all the questioning was done among those of our own side of the divide, very few answers appeared. This was the way things were and always would be. It may be difficult today for our modern minds to understand these attitudes. To find something of an equivalent, we have only to look at the attitudes across the divide of color in South Africa up to about a decade ago and remember that very few could imagine a different state of affairs.

Perhaps this is a good point at which to try to describe another element in the subtle walls that stood between us. I have used the terms Protestant and Catholic, fully aware of the nuances that others would wish to bring to both of these terms. The fact is that in the Ireland of my childhood and youth, there was no room for nuance. Next to the huge sea of Roman Catholicism, given that Irish Catholicism was probably the most resolute and unyielding in the church, any other tradition was so vulnerable that it tended to see itself as allied with anything that was not Roman Catholic!

Furthermore, the issue was far more complex than merely one of religion. As in many older societies, religion, culture, lifestyle, class, education, and even language were all bound together. Many Roman Catholics assumed that to be truly Irish, one could not be other than Roman Catholic in religion, nationalist or republican in politics, and supportive of an indigenous Irish culture that would be ideally expressed in a revitalized Irish language called Gaelic.

For most Protestants this created difficulties. The reasons for this lie in history and are therefore complex. Most Protestant families did not come from England and many of them had never been there, nor did they particularly wish to live there. However, they regarded English institutions like the monarchy, the Church of England, and English literature—much of it, ironically, written by gifted Anglo-Irish writers!—as in some sense theirs. After all, it was hardly a generation since the occupying British had left in 1923, and the vast majority of Protestants would not have been in favor of a free and independent republic. Many more affluent Protestant families had to some degree felt the threat of the republican forces, what would soon be called the Irish Republican Army.

Many of the "big houses," as the large estates were called, had been burned and their families had gone to England even though they may not have lived there for many generations, if ever. Many Protestant families would have had links with the British armed forces during the First World War; many would have sent their children to be educated in English schools. The Church of Ireland looked to Canterbury if not as a mother church, certainly as a sister. In the Second World War many prominent, high-ranking officers in the British forces were Irish, including a disproportionate number of generals. In the last two generations members of a single Church of Ireland family known to me, the Pikes, have been Bishop of Meath in Ireland, Bishop of Gambia in West Africa, Chaplain General of the British Army, Minister of Lands in Tanganyika, and Governor of British Somalia. In the present generation two sons are Anglican priests in western Canada; one daughter serves in the diocese of Yukon, and another is a doctor in Johannesburg.

When I was growing up, to be Protestant in the south of Ireland was to have your otherwise friendly Roman Catholic neighbors or professional colleagues assume that you and they had different loyalties. After all, we were together as citizens of a newly born republic, yet my Roman Catholic neighbor had only to look in the Church of Ireland's Book of Common Prayer to see the petition "O Lord, save the King" as the daily or weekly petition of Anglicans. It is an indication of the very reasonable attitude of the new national parliament that it did not pressure the Church of Ireland to consider changing this for many years. When it did so, the Church of Ireland responded by making a change that was jesuitical in its subtlety, so that the petition became, "O Lord, guide and defend our rulers."

As a young adult I felt caught between two worlds. My family name indicated quite undeniably that whether or not I was Anglican, my father's family had been Irish and Roman Catholic and had lived in Ireland for untold generations. The ruins of an abbey built by the family on its profits from piracy and smuggling stood on Sherkin Island in Bantry Bay on the borders of the counties of Cork and Kerry. To this day someone of the clan seems to run a pub or small store in every small town in the area! Our branch alone of the family had become Church of Ireland sometime in the nineteenth century, but all I have ever been able to find out about it is that it was not the result of a mixed marriage in which the Roman Catholic partner became Church of Ireland, because there were already children when the change was made. My guess is that the couple and their children became involved in a very late wave of Wesleyan revival that came to the southwest of the country and resulted in their conversion, thus moving into the world of Protestantism by way of the largest Protestant community around them—the Church of Ireland.

All of this history seems to come together in the story of my Aunt Hettie, my grandfather's sister. I remember her as incredibly wrinkled, bent over, and for some reason mysterious and formidable. She lived some distance away in another part of the town, in a house that was small and old and with lace curtains at the windows that were always closed. To enter it, which I think I did once in my life, was to encounter shadows, dark furniture, ancient dark green plants. I was able to sense that neither the family nor Aunt Hettie approved of one another and to my knowledge she never came to our house. I think I would have remembered such a visit, just as a child would remember if Queen Victoria came by one day!

In later life I learned that Aunt Hettie was outside the circle of the family because she had remained Roman Catholic, and yet she was not quite outside. She had been married once, but one got the impression of a bereavement early in their marriage. Whoever her husband was, he had faded away from the family circle in the vague and undefined way in which characters in a modern soap opera are written out of the script, hang ghostlike around the action for a little while, and then are gone. Aunt Hettie survived him, and in her relationship with our family there lay all the ambiguity and complexity of feelings and behavior that characterized the religious divide in that little world.

Aunt Hettie and the family were at one and the same time united and divided. They held the past in common, but each jealously guarded the present from the other. They stood on both sides of a gulf, rather as members of a tribe do when some have crossed over and the rest have chosen not to. They were certainly not enemies, but close friendship was impossible.

Even here there were contradictions, however, because when Aunt Hettie was ill we would visit her and bring her a basket of delicacies to eat. This readiness to live with contradiction, to allow personal relationships and kinship precedence over social and religious differences, made it possible for southern Ireland to be a place of greater harmony than its northern neighbor. "After all," as people used to say, "blood is thicker than water."

zebedee's children

My mother left her parents' farm in 1926 and came to Cork City to nurse. Here she and my father met and married, settling in the city where he and his family had "always" been. Later, when we three boys had been born, we lived in a house that was about a hundred and fifty yards from the parish church. Beside the church there was the rectory, a large Irish-Georgian house set in its own grounds. Between it and our house was the parish school. It had two large classrooms and two playgrounds, senior and junior, and a staff of two.

I arrived at the door of the junior school slightly before my fifth birthday, my hand firmly placed in that of my mother. There in the outer porch, its two rows of hooks holding the coats of my companions-to-be, we were met by Miss Buckley, a formidable figure to a four-year-old. I often try to imagine Miss Buckley as she would look to me today if we were to meet, but all my efforts are set to naught by the images of childhood. She was tall, if only because all adults are tall to a child, and she wore the most beautiful green woollen dress I had ever seen. Her massive gold brooch drew her rich brown hair back in a

chignon, the pin piercing its depths and reemerging
to engage the clasp. The brooch shone and flashed as
she turned her head or walked away from us toward
the blackboard. She also had graceful brown shoes
and a deep, pleasantly low voice. Even as I write
these lines I am intrigued at how vividly this woman
from long ago comes back to me.

You would think from all this that I could continue
to describe our first encounter with equal rapture.
Far from it. I tugged unwillingly on my mother's
arm, beginning at the iron gate of the playground
and continuing to the door of the red-tiled porch,
and then I threw myself on the floor in front of the
two women, kicking and screaming. I was still kicking and screaming as my mother took Miss Buckley's
advice and left. Then a warm and soft hand clasped
itself in mine, gently but most firmly. A low voice
communicated absolute authority to me in words I
have long since forgotten, if in fact I ever heard
them, and I was inside, meeting the eyes of my con-
temporaries, about to begin my first day at school.

At my place in the front row of small desks, I was
given something to play with that I had never seen
before and found totally captivating. It was a huge
toy boat, an ark, full of animals. I was encountering
my first great story, handling it, feeling it, entering
into it. To this day I think of that moment as the beginning of a love affair with the great narrative of
Holy Scripture.

In ways that are very difficult to understand today,
at the school the world of Scripture and of things religious in general was given precedence over everything else. The rector of the parish was also the

chairman of the school and he would appear in the classroom from time to time. My memory is that there was no particular regularity to his appearances—he would quite simply arrive. The teacher would have had a few minutes warning because the rectory driveway could be seen from the school windows. This vantage point, coupled with the fact that the rector walked extremely slowly with the help of a heavy walking stick, allowed a little leeway for preparation. When the rector eventually appeared at the door, everyone stood up—this gesture of respect was so automatic that no order was necessary. There would be a great clatter of desks as the seats fell back in their iron slots. The rector would exchange some pleasantries with Miss Buckley. After this we would be told to sit and the rector would speak to us or ask us some questions or give us something to learn.

The rector was extremely fond of the Old Testament. This, together with his flair for drama, ensured him a rapt audience. I realize now that he loved tales of action and conflict, or maybe in his wisdom he realized that we children would. More than once we heard the walls of Jericho come crashing down with shouting and the blowing of imagined trumpets. In those days an archdeacon wore the traditional clerical buttoned leggings and apron. To have our rector, thus clad, regale us with the story of Moses striking the rock in anger, the rector's black and silver-handled walking stick flailing at the front desk, his voice trembling with passion, was an experience never to be forgotten.

Through such encounters we received a strong implicit message about where real authority lay and what school subjects took precedence over everything else. History or arithmetic or English grammar might be important, but the "Duty toward God" passage of the church's catechism was quite obviously of more importance. Certainly that is what my child's mind got from these sessions.

Eventually there would come a day when Miss Buckley would make a most solemn announcement. It appeared that we had been put on notice that we were about to receive a visit from no less than the Diocesan Examiner. This august official was, I now surmise, a semi-retired priest whose duty it was to go around the diocesan parish schools examining the quality of the religious education being given. Following this news the rector would appear for even longer periods and Miss Buckley would set aside times from other subjects to concentrate on such things as the catechism, certain New Testament passages, and some psalms and Old Testament stories.

The time would arrive for the visitation. The figure of the Diocesan Examiner would appear crossing the playground, and great excitement would ensue. Miss Buckley would hastily pat her hair, smooth her dress, and move to the door. We children would be both frightened and excited—frightened because we were expected to answer correctly whatever was asked of us, and excited because it was well known that unless our performance was abysmal, the examiner would announce a half-day's holiday.

Canon Stewart—for that was his name—I remember as a frail, white-haired man with red rosy cheeks, a high excited voice, and many gesticulations, but above all with a merry twinkle in his eye. Very often when I have seen department store Santa Clauses with my children, and more recently with my grandchildren, I see and hear Canon Stewart again. He had a great capacity for laughter, something that belied the sonorities of his official title. He would examine us in the Bible stories we were being taught daily and would check on how well we were learning our catechism by heart. Delighting in sudden catch questions, he would wave the Bible in the air, extend a bony finger in someone's direction, and boom out: "Who was the father of Zebedee's children?" Since Miss Buckley, a veteran of many of these visits, knew that this question would inevitably be asked, we would have been primed to answer in a joyous chorus: "Zebedee!" Then another catch question would come: "Who wrote the Gospel according to Saint Mark?" To which we would quite naturally shout out triumphantly, "Saint Mark!"

Then the voice of Canon Stewart would change and his face would become more serious. He would point to one of us and ask, "What is your name?" We knew then that we had moved from the Bible to the catechism. The child he had pointed to would stand—you always stood when asked a question—and repeat his or her Christian names, all of them. We knew that the next question would be, "Who gave you this name?" and the reply would roll off our tongue with the ease of countless recitations: "My godfathers and godmothers in my baptism, wherein I was made a member of Christ, the child of God, and an inheritor of the Kingdom of Heaven." The examiner, with great emphasis on each phrase, would tell us that we must realize that the catechism was not telling us that we were merely *a* child of God. By no means. Each one of us—at this juncture he would look for a moment at each one of us—was nothing less than *the* child of God, special, unique, and beyond price.

Sitting in that schoolroom long ago, I could not know the immense wisdom in the simple words of this kind, elderly priest. I could not know that they expressed a timeless wisdom about the human need to possess what decades later would be called one's "personal story" or a sense of personal identity. I could not know that within my own lifetime a culture and a society would evolve in which the human spirit would feel itself isolated from its roots and sent to search anxiously and desperately for identity and story and meaning. In the far-off culture of the 1990s, millions of people would pay large sums of money and sacrifice endless hours to seek guidance in their quest after their true identity. With the help of psychiatrists, psychologists, therapists, and counselors of every conceivable quality and description, they would try to recall their past and share their present feelings and experiences, so that they could at last become people of hope and possess a liveable future. Yet every one of these elements in the human longing for personal identity and self-discovery lay hidden in the deceptively simple words of this catechism. I am a member of Christ—my origin and my past by baptism. I am the child of God—my assurance of being loved and valued beyond price. I am an inheritor of the kingdom of God—my symbol for hoping my way into the future.

After the catechism would come a testing of what we had been learning by heart. In those days, learning by rote was still a major element in our formation. Entirely apart from the scriptures and the prayer book, we would do a great deal of learning by rote in English literature.

The Diocesan Examiner would point at someone and ask for the thirteenth chapter of Paul's first letter to the Corinthians. The chosen person would stand and launch into Paul's hymn to love, eventually stopping at some point and having to be prompted, or arriving successfully and triumphantly at the end of the chapter, to be praised effusively by our visitor. Other passages frequently requested were the nativity story in Luke's Gospel, various great passages of Isaiah's prophecy, the lament of David for Saul and Jonathan, various passages from the Gospel according to John, Paul's exhortation to put on the armor of God—to name a few. Then we might move on to passages of the prayer book we had learned by heart: many of the collects, some great passages of the psalms, most of the catechism. All these would be recited with varying degrees of skill, accompanied by prompting for our failures and praise for our successes.

Today many would question this whole exercise. All I can say in its defense is that by this rote learning I was given a kind of personal, portable golden treasury that has served me well ever since, and that has made Scripture as normal a part of my consciousness as Shakespeare's *Hamlet* or Virgil's *Aeneid* or Grimm's *Fairy Tales*—or, for that matter, any part whatsoever of the vast world of the humanities.

Because Miss Buckley remains in my memory as a figure of singular self-control, I recall an occasion when that self-control forsook her. It was on one of the visits of the Diocesan Examiner that this awe-inspiring—at least to us children—display of emotion took place. For some reason we had done her anything but credit on this particular occasion. My own dismal contribution was to launch out into the parable of the talents when the question had referred to the laborers in the vineyard. All in all it was a grim afternoon. Even Canon Stewart's usually benign expression began to look a trifle strained. Before he left he chatted quietly to Miss Buckley, the two of them standing by the entrance some distance from us. When the door finally closed behind him and the click of the iron gate told her that he was across the playground and so out of earshot, she turned to speak to us. She began quietly, but by the time she had finished, her face was flushed and she dabbed at her eyes with a snow-white lace handkerchief.

The helpless misery of that afternoon returns to me whenever either of those parables reappears in the three-year lectionary. On those Sundays I appear to others to be a mature cleric celebrating the liturgy. In reality I am once again an eight-year-old schoolboy hunkered down in my desk as the wrath of Miss Buckley swirls and thunders around me. When I choose to do a homily on either of these parables, I do my best to make it a good one as a vain offering to her memory, seeking to undo my betrayal of her on that awful day!

the old tongue

The Gaelic word for a steamship, spelled phonetically in English letters, is *gollthawn*. At six years old I know this word because Miss Buckley has begun to direct our attention to a large glossy poster hanging on the schoolroom wall. On this poster are about a score of common, everyday things: a house, a donkey, a bus, and—complete with a small white bow wave and blue wake—a steamship.

I recall the steamship most clearly of all, perhaps because it hinted of far-off places. Steamships like this one would plough up and down the river where I was taken for afternoon walks or rides on my tricycle. On their way down from the docks and out to sea they would pass the battlemented tower of the castle at Blackrock, hooting mournfully as they rounded the wide bend in the river, bound for the harbor and the open ocean beyond. Sometimes as I lay awake in bed the sound of a ship's horn would come across the darkened city, at times strong or faint as the wind changed and played with it, and I would wonder what it must be like heading out to sea instead of staying warm and secure in one's own bed and home. So it was that the first Gaelic word familiar to me was *gollthawn*. For all I know, it may have been the liquid and haunting sound of that word that began a love of the language.

For some days—or was it weeks?—Miss Buckley turned us to the wall hanging. After awhile each object began to have a story, some more than one story. Miss Buckley would encourage us to tell them, allowing us to embroider them with each telling. Then there came the day when she made an exciting announcement. We were going to receive our first Irish language reader. It was the autumn of 1934.

In her own way Miss Buckley was a dramatist of high order. She knew how to milk such occasions for utmost effect. New books were always an event. When we came in on the great morning the small pile would already be impeccably arranged on her table. At this point she would not merely pick them up and distribute them; each book was lifted separately and taken to a particular child. Miss Buckley would then open it at the first lesson, running her immaculately manicured finger down the spine of the book, the pink skin of her hand always slightly whitened by chalk dust. Then she would return to the front, pick up another book, and go to another child. Whether or not this was her purpose, she communicated to us a love of books as objects, as well as the feeling of having received, not just a book, but our own particular book, and even receiving it as a kind of prize to be treasured.

When my book had been placed on my desk with this ceremony, I saw on the opened page a large, brightly colored picture. Two people—a young Celtic warrior armed with a spear and battle axe and a beautiful young woman gowned and cloaked, her long hair golden—stood together on the shore of a shining sea. In the distance was a fort (or *dun* as it would be called in Gaelic), and in the foreground, just offshore as if waiting to bear them away, stood a ship with a single large sail. Forests clothed the surrounding low hills. I was looking at the Ireland of the ninth century, suitably romanticized for my generation, the first generation of a new Irish Free State.

Irish Gaelic is one member of a small family of languages that used to be spoken, and to a very small extent still are, on the western edge of Europe. There are two main branches: Irish and Scottish Gaelic are similar, as are Welsh and Breton. There is little similarity between the two branches. To my knowledge the latter is found only in Normandy and Brittany. Welsh is the one exception to my saying that these languages used to be spoken: a very large proportion of Welsh people have a command of their language and it is still especially rich in poetry, song, and literature. I was taught Gaelic from the age of six, and eventually I myself taught it, having kept it as one of my subjects in university.

As a living language, Irish Gaelic came under attack in the late seventeenth century. At that time English military power broke the resistance of the old Irish landowning families and forced many to flee the country, some of them ending their days as emigres in the various Catholic lands of Europe and South America. Laws were then imposed with the intention of destroying once and for all Irish Catholic identity and power. From then on the language ceased to be used except as the tongue of an increasingly impoverished and desperate peasant population. In 1829 these laws were repealed, only to be followed by the horrors of the potato famine in the 1840s that triggered the massive emigration flood to the United States and Canada.

In 1923, in a brutal and bloody upheaval, the new Irish state was declared and the tasks of building a nation began. One of the early slogans was *Tir fan teanga tir gan duthchaish*, which in English means roughly, "A country without its language is a country without a true soul." The decision was made to do what the nation of Israel also set out to do about the same time—to revive a language that had ceased to be a language of everyday living. While there was no real hope—or wish—that the English language and culture would be banished from Irish life, it was hoped that every Irish child would have two languages, as well as a full acquaintance with Irish history, culture, art, and literature.

My generation entered school at the end of the first decade of this attempt at revival. In almost all Protestant schools the program was seen as an imposition, unrealistic, and unnecessary. George Bernard Shaw remarked with typical acidity that the Irish people were trying to exchange a language that gave them command of three-quarters of the globe for one that gave them command of a cabbage patch! However, the lure of government grants for every student studying Irish Gaelic was too much even for Protestant schools to resist.

For some reason, I liked learning Irish Gaelic from the beginning. Who knows why? In a way I couldn't realize then but now see clearly, the language was saturated with a natural sense of the presence of God in every aspect of life—sleep and waking, love and battle, joy and sorrow, life and death. I was in touch with a language that had died before either the Enlightenment of the eighteenth century or the Industrial Revolution of the nineteenth had touched its thought forms and assumptions. In this sense Irish Gaelic was giving me the same gifts as Scripture. Each spoke and told and sang of a world in which Jacob's ladder still linked heaven and earth. Its world was one world, not a world split in two, as was already happening in western culture.

It was also a world that had an unquestioned place for the church, Christian faith, and the priest. One of the great ironies of all Irish literature, whether it is encountered in Irish Gaelic, in English translations of Gaelic, or in Anglo-Irish writers in English, is that even where the writing is anticlerical—and much of it is—it always seems to assume implicitly that the church and the faith and the priest will always be around to rail against! To the Irish mind it was impossible to conceive of a world without them.

Learning Irish Gaelic as a Protestant child also allowed me to enter at least the outskirts of a mysterious country all around me but one that I could never enter—the world of Roman Catholicism. For instance, my own church taught me an uncompromising reticence toward the Virgin Mary. Certainly, we were told, she was our Lord's virgin mother, but I was most certainly never to be caught praying to her or through her. Such were the admonitions of Sunday school, confirmation class, and, later, university theology lectures. Yet amid all these admonitions, I would also be learning a simple Irish Gaelic poem which, in translation, reads:

> O Mary of Grace
>> Mother of the Son of God,
> May you direct me
>> For my good.
>
> May you save me
>> From every evil,
> May you preserve me
>> Body and Soul.
>
> God of the angels
>> Above my head,
> God before me
>> And God beside me.

So it was, in this and in many other texts, that the language linked my consciousness to the dominant Christianity of the island.

The same was true for links between the language and the emerging nationalist politics of Ireland. My Protestant tradition would link me naturally with things English, with English literature and a sense of relationship to the Church of England, but here again Irish literature in Gaelic would act with a certain subversion. There is a genre of poetry in Irish Gaelic that became popular in the late seventeenth and eighteenth centuries, those centuries when it was very dangerous to be heard speaking out politically. These poems, highly lyrical and romantic, were called *Aisling* (pronounced "Ashling"). They were conventional in form and always followed a strict pattern. In every one a beautiful young woman (Ireland) is threatened by a rich, strong bully (England). She is looking desperately for help from a noble and handsome prince who is, alas, far away. The prince is always a symbol for either France or Spain, the two great Catholic powers of Europe at the time. The best-known poem in this genre is called, in its English translation, "My Dark Rosaleen."

> O my dark Rosaleen,
>   Do not sigh, do not weep,
> The priests are on the ocean blue,
>   They march along the deep.
>
> There's wine from the royal Pope,
>   And Spanish ale to give you hope,
> To give you life and joy and hope,
>   O my dark Rosaleen.

The language kept up a quiet invitation to link together all the disparate pieces of our lives, cultural, political, and religious, and to become truly and completely Irish. Again, because the language had never been affected by the Enlightenment or the Industrial Revolution, and because the Ireland of my childhood was still rural and agrarian, Irish literature, whether written in Gaelic or in English, resonated with a deep, unbroken relationship to the sanctity of the created order. Very often I and other children would stand in the classroom and recite such lines as these, written by Joseph Mary Plunkett, an Irish poet who died in the rebellion of 1916:

I see His blood upon the rose,
And in the stars the glory of His eyes,
His body gleams amid eternal snows,
His tears fall from the skies.

I see His face in every flower;
The thunder and the singing of the birds
Are but His voice—and carven by His power
Rocks are His written words.

All pathways by His feet are worn,
His strong heart stirs the ever-beating sea,
His crown of thorns is twined with every thorn,
His cross is every tree.

I sometimes think that adult life is a vast echo chamber for the voices of childhood, a vast screen on which reflections of the past are captured in unexpected moments. Many years after Miss Buckley presided over us, pointing with infinite patience to the hanging chart of familiar things, the long-forgotten word *gollthawn* came back suddenly and hauntingly as I sat watching David Lean's movie *Ryan's Daughter*. The story is set in the early twentieth century in the west of Ireland, and one of the central characters, played by Robert Mitchum, is the village schoolteacher. In a scene in the little school, there behind Mitchum on the wall hung the identical government-issued poster of that time. There, too, was my steamship, sailing back to me across time, its bow wave white, its wake blue, its black funnel belching smoke.

the door

Choir practice is on Wednesdays at four o'clock. Classes in the parish school next to the church end at three o'clock, so we have a precious hour in which to play. When we come in just before four—we would not dare be late—Mr. Garrett, the choirmaster, is always there before us and it is unthinkable that he would not be. Let me introduce you to him.

He is a small man in stature, not much taller than we choirboys, who vary in age from seven to fourteen years old. Because he is small, Mr. Garrett needs to be very fierce and every one of us is afraid of him. He has a round, pink face framed by white hair at the sides and nothing on top. He rolls his own cigarettes, which are pathetic, hastily assembled things with tobacco hanging from both ends. He smokes incessantly and there is always a cigarette hanging from his lower lip at the lefthand side, even when he is singing. For some reason enshrined only in some obscure law of gravity it stays there; I have no memory of it ever dropping. To this day certain great anthems of the church bring to my inner eye not only the wondrous images of which they sing—archangels and shepherds and heavenly choirs—but the even more wondrous defiance of the law of gravity achieved by Mr. Garrett and his hand-rolled cigarettes.

He sits behind a huge black grand piano that stands in the center of the choir room. In front of him and beside him there are two long prayer desks with chairs where we sit. It is essential that Mr. Garrett keep every single one of us in sight all the time, and to make this possible he always perches on top of three or four large service books. To this day the very words *Te Deum by Stanford in F* represent for me not only one of the great church canticles, but also one of the layers of books on Mr. Garrett's chair and one of the necessary elements in his authority.

In those days choir practice could be a very serious affair. At a certain stage in Handel's *Messiah* there is a high C for a soprano. It comes during the recitative of the nativity story and sings of "a multitude of the heavenly host praising God and saying...." Today whenever I sit in some theater or cathedral and the performance is approaching this point, all the massive choirs and soloists disappear for me. Instead, Mr. Garrett, almost apoplectic with rage, climbs down from his precariously piled chair, advances on one of the senior choir boys, and proceeds to bang him around the head with the large black score of the *Messiah* because he has just failed to reach high C.

The choir room was in the crypt of the church and it smelled of age. The prayer desks had the names of previous choirboys cut into the wood. We could never understand when they had had the time or the opportunity to do this, since it was obvious that Mr. Garrett would annihilate any boy he caught. One could only assume that at some time in the past there had been a kinder, gentler choirmaster who either tolerated the vandalism or was helpless to prevent it from happening.

Around the walls stood tall cupboards for the robes of the boys and the men. The floor was bare wood, with knots that made it uneven. In the corner of the room I remember a very ancient door, rather low, pointed at the top and with a black iron handle. When you opened it—which wasn't easy and could be done only when Mr. Garrett was out of the room and someone was posted as lookout—you saw the first two or three steps of a dark, winding staircase, a layer of dust, and some large cobwebs. We were warned by Mr. Garrett never to venture into this area, an instruction that naturally had the effect of peopling that dark staircase to the tower with the most ghoulish and frightful possibilities.

Why do I share with you such ordinary memories? Because they are part of a greater whole. Mr. Garrett, perched on his pile of service books, his cigarette dangling, his wrath as terrible as an army with banners, was also the one who opened doors to a wonderful and beautiful world. Looking back, I realize now that the small, mysterious door in the corner of the choir room was a magic door opening onto the world of great church music. I owe to Mr. Garrett the great oratorios and the finest settings of the church's canticles. I owe him Mary's *Magnificat*, Simeon's *Nunc Dimittis*, Isaiah's *Urbs Fortitudinis*, and a score of others. I owe him the *Benedicite*, that great and thrilling song of whales and ice and snow and creeping things, all of them together praising the Lord decades before the first environmentalist was heard from or the Sierra Club was formed. I owe him the high, clear cadences of *Veni Creator* spilling out across the green grounds of the rectory and on into the wood on the other side of the hill, falling away from the church down to my home. I owe him the thunder of "Saint Patrick's Breastplate" and the sharp, infinitely haunting intervals of old Irish tunes carrying newer and younger English words.

Sometime late in the sixth century Saint Columba wrote in the Latin of his time:

> Beyond our ken thou shinest,
> The everlasting light,
> Ineffable in loving,
> Unthinkable in might.
>
> Thou to the meek and lowly
> Thy secrets dost unfold.
> O God, thou knowest all things,
> All things both new and old.
>
> I walk secure and blessed
> In every clime and coast,
> In name of God the Father,
> And Son, and Holy Ghost.

Here is the authentic voice of Celtic spirituality, simple in expression, mystical in its understanding of God, restless in its urge to explore "every clime and coast." Columba wrote these words in his cell on Iona, not half a mile from where the cold, blue-green waters of the Atlantic wash on the stony shore. I, a child of some fifteen centuries in his future, sang it on winter afternoons against the crying of gulls and the sad wail of distant foghorns warning of the dangers of the same nearby Atlantic.

In front of the church four roads intersected at what was called Saint Luke's Cross. At the center of the intersection stood a stone trough full of water. Although by 1937 some motorcars and buses passed through that intersection, there still were many horse-drawn carts. Here at this trough the horses would come to drink before continuing to pull their heavy burdens. After choir practice on winter evenings, when dusk had sufficiently fallen and the last shops were beginning to put out their lights, we choirboys would rush from practice toward the horse trough. Almost by instinct two groups would form and the first group to reach the trough would claim possession of it. It was the task of the others to take it from them. The price of a successful attack on the fortress of the enemy was to be half-drowned by the water hurled by the defenders. Eventually, soaking wet and exhilarated by the battle, we would head for home to face the wrath of our parents.

One night stands out in my memory. The sky is clear—unusual in Ireland in midwinter—and the stars are glitteringly pure. I am breathless, cold, wet, and tired, yet I feel utterly alive as I head for home. The voices of the others, calling out to each other either muffled taunts or plans for the next day, grow fainter and fainter as we all scatter to our various homes. It is very near Christmas—it must be, because we have just been practicing Gustav Holst's incomparable tune to Christina Rossetti's words. I am heading for home, half walking, half running, gasping with the breathlessness that is both exertion but also the joy of being alive. Under the clear, cold evening sky a voice, my own but also the voices of many others, sings:

> In the bleak midwinter,
> > frosty wind made moan,
> Earth stood hard as iron,
> > water like a stone;
> Snow had fallen,
> > snow on snow,
> > > snow on snow,
> In the bleak midwinter,
> > long ago.

a dream of white mountains

When I think of the bedroom my brother and I shared for a number of our growing years, I realize that the very act of remembering makes everything seem larger than it really was. I suspect, therefore, that our room was quite small, with a double bed, a wardrobe, a mat for our feet when we got out of bed, a small bedside table, and a dressing table that must have been an exile from my parents' bedroom. The bedroom also had a bay window and that most wonderful of all things—a bedroom fireplace. When we were ill with the various diseases of childhood, the most luxurious of gifts was to have a fire lit in the bedroom. It would have been a coal fire, damped down with wet, pulverized coal called "slack" that kept the fire going for many hours. It never blazed up, but glowed through the long, slow hours of the afternoon. As the daylight died, I could lay on my side and gaze drowsily into the fire, knowing that very soon a tray would appear with suitably gentle and tempting foods for a passing childhood malady.

Our room also had a bay window with its own windowsill where we could sit and feel that we were outside while we were still inside the room. There was a space there to put our toys. Whether I was there alone or together with my brother or my friends, there was always a pool of sunlight to sit in or the spattering of rain on the glass next to my ear so close that I could feel I was out in it, but no one was shouting for me to come in.

My younger brother and I shared that double bed and that room for three or four years. Then in my memory a crib suddenly appears in the far corner, and soon my father enters in a kind of remembered dream and tells us that we have a little brother. Sometime after that I move to another room, the only other bedroom in the house, and have a room of my own. But just before the crib appears I have a long, shadowy period in that room. It was the summer of 1937, when my brother could not be with me and I occupied a very solitary world in which the only other people were my parents and the doctor.

Early that summer I came down with the kind of infection that is easily cured today, but in those days before antibiotics was very serious for children. To treat scarlet fever and septicemia, isolation was called for. My brother moved out of the room and a large sheet was hung on the door, a sheet soaked daily in some kind of disinfectant I can no longer name. That sheeted door became the limit of my world for most of that summer, about nine weeks in all. From time to time the doctor would come, a small, overweight man who puffed as he ascended the stairs to my room. He would talk to me in a wheezy but friendly voice, and when he sat on the edge of my bed and touched me, I would get a scent of something medicinal—clean, fresh, official, and authoritative. My mother was a nurse, so she and he would have conversations about me just out of earshot.

Then began the delicious part of that long bedridden summer. I began to discover, and then to indulge, an obsessive love of reading. Up to that point my parents had criticized me for reading comic books—"penny dreadfuls" they were called in those days. My parents' attitude to comics seemed contradictory to me because I noticed that, in other moods, my father spoke nostalgically of the favorite reading of his childhood and it sounded suspiciously like the comics and weekly boys' papers that I was discovering! But this was the summer that everything changed. Because they realized I was dangerously ill, they treated me to a feast of weekly boys' papers; it was a dream come true. I could not lend them to anyone for fear of infection, so I would devour one and lay it aside only to have it replaced by another, crisp and bright, right off the large magazine and newspaper stand at the nearby railway station.

From these weekly papers I moved to slightly longer stories in smaller and thicker booklets. They had names like *The Boys' Library, The Adventure Library*, and *The Sexton Blake Library*. On the back cover would be an endless list of all the titles in the series I had yet to read. Heaven on earth! This too was the summer I discovered science fiction, tales of wonderful adventures on board rockets to the planet Venus. But what I remember best is the day when my father came in bearing what seemed an enormous book. It was a copy of *CHUMS ANNUAL*, subtitled *A Book for the Boys of the Empire*. Even now, as I write this title my instinct is to print it in capital letters! The book was so enormous and so wonderful. It had hundreds of pages, scores of stories and articles, features and jokes—terrible jokes, as I recall—endless designs and plans for making things, even some poems and heaven knows now what else.

Years later on a rainy day in Vancouver I was passing a very good rare and used bookshop not far from the cathedral where I was dean. There in the window was a copy of an old *Chums Annual!* In a moment I was inside, handing over an exorbitant sum without the slightest protest. I would have given my life savings for this book. It was exactly the same volume I had been given in that summer of 1937, and as I opened and smelled the pages it was as though I had entered a time warp.

By August of that childhood summer I was very ill. There was not much the doctor could do beyond care and watchful concern. One afternoon I heard the rector's voice in the downstairs hall; because of the dread of contagion he did not come up to me. I knew that he had come to offer a special prayer with my parents.

One night in particular was full of nightmares. Because I was delirious and thrashing about, my mother threw her fur coat over me on top of the blankets. Then I had a vivid dream. I was being pursued by a wolf in the forest and could not run fast enough to get away. I woke up shouting and calling, gripping the fur coat collar, with my father lying beside me keeping me wrapped in warm clothes. Very late at night the doctor came to examine me and the room was full of tension and alarm, and after that I remember sunlight and a fresh morning and a tray brought by my mother. As we said in those days, my fever had broken and I had come through.

Then began the weeks of recovery, when I read and read. Someone gave me John Oxenham's *The Hidden Years*, a book about the boy Jesus in his growing years, and I discovered the Martian chronicles of H. Rider Haggard, who called the planet by the far more romantic name Pellucidar. I found Kenneth Graham's *The Wind in the Willows* and "the piper at the gates of dawn," which has always been for me a shining example of the presence of the numinous Other in our lives.

Finally came the wonderful day when I was given permission to leave the room. Although I had to stay upstairs, I could go into the front room—my parents' bedroom—and look out on the street. That summer our whole street was being repaved, so there was a good deal to look at. A little later on, I was allowed to open the window and lean out and talk to one of my friends, who had just received a wonderful present from America. For an Irish child in those days, the word "America" meant great distances, wonder, inventions, cowboys, Hollywood, Al Capone, the Empire State Building, Prince Valiant, Superman....Even now the heady list makes me breathless. My friend said he would lend me the present, and so I saw and handled my first Viewmaster, with its eight round disks of tiny colored transparencies. You slid each one into the viewer, looked in through the eyepieces, and saw a crystal-clear and vivid scene in three dimensions. I never got tired of going through that box sent from faraway America.

Those simple pictures triggered a dream that had an uncanny power in my life. Among the Viewmaster slides were a number of the Rockies, both American and Canadian. At the time, the very words "Rocky Mountains" rang with infinite romance. I looked at the pictures again and again, that faraway world so utterly different from the small, circumscribed view of terraced houses and small walled gardens from my bedroom window. Here through these magic casements I looked at skies impossibly blue, the snow-crowned mountain peaks calling me to reach out and touch them. One night I dreamed that I was traveling toward them. The long range in the distance got nearer and nearer. Then, in the way that dreams do, everything was gone and I awoke.

I could not know then, in my childhood room, that many years in the future I would be driving with my wife Paula and our children toward those same mountains, that we would come over a rise in the foothills country of Alberta only to see ahead of us a blue, white-topped wall of rock filling the horizon from north to south. In that same moment I held in my hand once again the small Viewmaster, heard again the clicking of its disk of tiny transparencies, and saw again the vivid images whose reality I was about to enter.

secret places

It is the summer of 1938 and we are in Donaguile, my grandfather's farm in Kilkenny. He and my two uncles are out in the field making hay with John, the hired man. My brother and I—he is six and I am ten—are standing on top of a ditch looking across toward the edge of the dark woods that stretch along the crown of this broad, gentle valley. These fields have been rented this year by our family so they are a few miles from our farm, higher up the side of the valley. Because of this, we boys have never been as near to the woods before; we have always seen them in the distance, a dark mysterious border to our universe.

Between us and the treeline lies a stretch of harsher land. Tough tangled grasses, wild flowers, bushes of various kinds, and nettles stand between us and the treeline, yet it calls us all the more to try to get there. We try to see a path through the undergrowth, and we know if we keep on talking about it, we will put off having to go forward. We are afraid without admitting it. We stand there, straining to pierce the shadows among the trees, wondering, imagining. For us the wood is the place where the known world ends, the border of a kingdom held by a mysterious ruler.

As our grandfather and uncles and John continue to work, we two boys have a contest to see who is brave enough to go alone to a point nearer the treeline. Each of us tries, hesitates, retreats, trots back to safety. As we do so our imagination becomes more and more feverish. We are preparing ourselves for an onslaught of wolves. Perhaps a dragon or trolls or goblins of some terrible kind will rush out and drag us screaming out of the sunlit world into the green silent darkness.

Even as we boys explore the imaginary world deep within our wood, a young man across the Irish Sea in Cambridge University is beginning to tell stories of a strange Norse world with briars and a wood and flying clouds and witches and spells and talking beasts and evil forces and a great Lion. He is forming these images because he has been brought up in this same kind of countryside some miles to the north on this same island. All his life he will like nothing better than walking in fields like this with a stout stick, his tweeds, his pipe, and a friend, feeling a light wind like this, seeing treetops like these bow from side to side under a cloudy sky. Later on in my life I will encounter this wood again, with its harsh barrier of briars that repels and attracts, in the pages of C. S. Lewis's books about the mythical land of Narnia.

About a mile to our left, beyond the east end of the wood, stands a grove of trees. It, too, is on the ridge of the hills. Once upon a time it was linked to the wood, both of them forming the great forest that clothed most of the country up to the fifteenth century. This area later became a golf course for the town merchants and others. From time to time I ven-

tured into the grove with my friend Paddy Byrne as
we looked for lost golf balls. As we entered slowly
there would be a breeze sighing in the higher
branches of the trees. Instinctively we would be silent. At the center of the grove was a clearing where
we could pick up a few balls discovered in the soft
mossy grass. Then I would want to leave, turning
away with that vague feeling of fear we all recall
from childhood when it is better not to look back and
see what might be coming after us. After that, I
would often look at the grove from the farmhouse,
seeing it outlined against the evening sky, the great
trees still as statues, the shadows of sunset lengthen-
ing, the warm light of the paraffin lamp being lit in
the kitchen, giving reassurance against the night.

Nearer the house, only about four fields away, was
a place we called the gullet. I don't know where the
name came from. The gullet was a sunken cavern
open to the sky. At one end a stream spilled in from
the field, falling about ten feet or so to form a large
pool on the floor of the cavern. This pool, about two
to three feet deep, in turn overflowed the surrounding circle of rocks and flowed toward the opposite
bank, where it disappeared in a natural tunnel.

My brother and I used to climb down into the gullet by a narrow, overgrown, sloping path. When we
were fully inside the whole world was filled with the
sound of the small waterfall splashing and tumbling
into the pool and the wind turning up the leaves of
what we called "sally trees." In a moment the trees
would cease to be green—they would seem to turn
white as they showed the underside of their leaves.
Ghostlike, they would shimmer for a moment until

the breeze died and they returned to their real color.
We returned there to play again and again in this en-
closed and magic world.

I often wonder if "magic" is the word our culture
uses for such places and times when it is wary of using the word "sacred." In that older world—or was it
a much younger world?—every field had a name, as
if the very field itself was a living thing. The gullet
was in the far corner of the field called "Back o' Brennan's." Next to this was "Darby's Haggart." Beyond
that was "Back o' Martin's." Beside the farmhouse itself was the "Barn Field," the "Hill Field" and, further
up the slope of the valley, the "Horse Field" and the
"Hayseed."

Leaving "Back o' Brennan's" we would come to
the place where that same stream, having stayed un-
derground for a few hundred yards, would reemerge
and drop down again, this time into an opening that
was deeper and longer. To get to this we scrambled
down an earthen path until we reached the floor of
what was really a small ravine. Again there was a waterfall, slightly higher and noisier than the previous
one, and again rocks formed a pool into which it fell.
This pool was deeper, so that when it overflowed its
rock barrier it flowed away faster and stronger. Here
we had to talk loudly to be heard. Here, too, we
would see a white shape moving under the water, its
arms outspread. It was the only shirt owned by John,
the hired man on the farm. Every week he came and
placed it here under a few heavy stones, letting the
stream wash it so it would be clean for Sunday Mass.
To a small boy it was far from being a mere shirt. At
different times it would become a ghost, a shark, a

whale, a dragon, a submarine, a monster, a dead body—according to the light, the shadows, the time of day, and my own fantasies.

We often went there. Sometimes I went alone when I became old enough to take a bucket to draw water from the well that was also in the ravine. The summer before I had been given a copy of Kenneth Graham's book *The Wind and the Willows,* with its chapter called "The Piper at the Gates of the Dawn." In it Mr. Mole and Mr. Rat are out rowing on the great river when they hear a mysterious piping that both draws and repels them, attracts and yet terrifies. When they finally arrive at the source of the mysterious and mesmerizing music, they find themselves in the presence of Pan. I remember wondering if that was the real reason I loved going to the deep pool with its waterfall and the dancing stream flowing under the branches of the sally trees that whispered when the wind stirred them.

Other places come back to me. Far away, infinitely far away in the mind of a child but actually quite near to our house in the city, there was a place called "the glen," a wide valley at the edge of the city bu' hidden from the eye by a row of houses. You wen down a sloping lane between the houses and there before you the land fell away in green ridges like steps to the valley floor. When you bounded down the slopes of green, lush grass you came to a small river that flowed through the glen. You could fish for minnows there, and when you tired and climbed the slope again you could look to the north and see a line of blue hills in the distance. They, too, formed the boundaries of my world. In that glen there was always sunshine and time never ended. Sometimes when I hear or speak of "eternal life," I suspect that it can be found in that long-ago glen, but, of course, only by a child.

I remember another sacred place, a very different kind of space: a cathedral echoing with song. Every year on the Feast of the Ascension the boys' choir of our parish would join the cathedral choir to sing Evensong. There was a vastness about the Cathedral of Saint Finbar, especially in the great marble-walled ambulatory that circled around behind the high altar. I remember one year, as we passed in procession, I saw a gleaming coffin beside a marble tomb. It was probably awaiting burial on the morrow, and to a choirboy it added an even greater measure of awe to the place and the occasion. Our voices in the psalm would cry out, "Who is the King of Glory?" and the men would shout in unison, "The Lord of Hosts, He is the King of Glory!" The organist would lift his arms in the air, bring them down on the keys, and the organ would thunder. I knew without any doubt that this vast, echoing pile of blue-grey stone, polished wood, gleaming brass, and shining stained glass windows was indeed a place of wonder and glory, well-fitted to be God's house.

But, of course, childhood has many moods, many ecstasies, and many fears. I read recently that the Japanese have a saying that until seven a child lives with the gods. There can be many kinds of gods, many different encounters with the sacred—beautiful and captivating, dark and terrifying, sometimes blended. For me such an encounter lay waiting in the quarry.

Even in daylight I never went near it. The entrance to the field in which the quarry lay had two stone pillars and an iron gate. Beside one of those pillars were steps to cross the low wall, what in those days was called a stile. From the top of the stile, just before one began to go down the other side into the forbidden field, one could see the quarry. It was a large, circular depression in the ground, probably about fifty yards in diameter. Because of its depth, magnified many times in a child's imagination, its water was always still and black. Around the steeply sloping edge of the water wet mud gleamed under the hooves of the cattle who scrambled down to drink on hot summer days, their slow, lazy movements making a soft squelching sound.

I had only to stand on the stile to feel that I was trespassing. All the voices of the family—parents, grandparents, uncles—sounded in my head. "You are never to go near the quarry," the voices said. I would stand there, my imagination working overtime. I would think of my uncle who had died when he was five. I had been named after him. I would wonder if he had disobeyed that rigid command, had ventured down that grassy slope, had felt his small feet sucked down by the mud...or did some vast thing rise from the inky water and take him down? Whereupon I would hastily clamber down from my forbidden perch and run toward the distant farmhouse, my feet splashing in the rain puddles in the baked clay of the narrow road.

One day in late summer, the family went to visit some relatives high up on the other side of the valley. For such a journey the horse and the large trap were prepared and harnessed, and rugs were thrown in for the night-time journey home. The adults clambered in and sat on the two long, cushioned seats facing each other. I stood in the well of the trap between them, my eyes just high enough to look along the wide haunches of the horse to where the silver of his saddle and bridle gleamed in the afternoon sun.

That night, the visit ended and goodbyes said, I dozed in the well of the trap, lying on a rug. Hours went by as the large vehicle creaked and swayed to the horse's trotting, the hard rubber rims of the wheels crunching the graveled roads. It was a clear night with a bright harvest moon almost full. As we climbed slowly up from the town to the farm we rounded the bend before the quarry gate. By this time awake and deliciously secure in the folds of the rug, I asked to be allowed to stand up for a moment so that I could see the quarry at night.

There it lay, blacker than I had ever imagined it could be, its surface utterly still. In the center of the black void was a great glowing eye, staring, pale, yellow, motionless, fearsome. I cowered in my uncle's arms, staying there until we turned into the driveway of the farm, to be welcomed home by my grandfather. No amount of adult explanation about the moon shining in the water would suffice to reassure me. I had seen what lay in the quarry, emerging at night into the darkened world as I slept.

Such were the many places I now know to have had for me the quality we call sacred. Naturally, such a naming of them would never have occurred to me at that time. Those places were no more and no less than places where for some reason one longed to be, where one had certain feelings that varied from fearfulness to a strange and undefinable joy. The adult I now am has learned to speak and to write of something called "sacred space," but, as with so many sacred things, one possessed them as a child long before one could name them. Come to think of it, the same may be true of all elements of God's grace.

sunday morning in the country

my grandfather's farm was on the side of a wide and gently sloping valley in County Kilkenny, about twelve miles from the ancient Norse city of that name. From a turn in the road at the end of our farmlands we could look down the slope of the fields and see the roofs of the small town of Castlecomer, the usual columns of smoke curling upward from the chimneys of the little houses. At times when the wind was right we could hear the sounds of the town's life—the buzzing of some machine, the infrequent honking of a car horn, the ringing of the angelus bell of the Church of the Immaculate Conception at six in the evening.

Another bell, smaller and further away on the other side of the town, was our call to worship. The Church of Saint Mary—an infrequent dedication in the Church of Ireland—stood on the crown of a slope amid the headstones of the generations that had worshiped within its walls. Every Sunday morning, softly but insistently and clearly, the sound of its bell would steal up through the fields and along the narrow roads to the farmhouse. Its first ring would be the signal for a number of things to happen. Either my uncle would run to harness the horse and trap— if a number of us were going, as was usual in the summer when we city visitors were around—or the donkey and trap if it was just himself, my aunt, and their oldest children. A third possibility, especially in the summer, was to go on bicycles. This precluded the youngest, and I can recall a delicious sense of having come of age the first summer I was allowed to bicycle to church with the rest of them.

That summer the ride to Saint Mary's is easy for me because it is downhill nearly all the way. The bicycles we have are heavy, black, tank-like Raleighs, the kind that Great Britain shipped for decades to the outer reaches of the empire. Along the earthen country road we go, avoiding the rain puddles that seemed to linger even on fine days, the cornfield on our right, then the hay field and the quarry field. I can free-wheel now for about half a mile, the wind in my face, a wonderful sense of freedom, the voice of my father or mother or uncle calling to me to be careful, not to get too far ahead. I pass the first of the "government cottages"—today we would call them subsidized housing—until I am at the first cross-roads, where I wait for the others to catch up. Here there are always a few people taking a rest, sitting on the low stone wall or leaning against a bicycle or holding the harness of a donkey or horse. If there is time we, too, pause, my aunt and uncle blending into the web of the conversations as any other neighbor would. Perhaps it's important to point out that almost all those whom we encounter on these morning rides to church are Roman Catholic, and they returning from one of the many Masses of the morning. We move among them as one of only four Church of Ireland families on that side road for many miles. But when we stop we are warmly welcomed, and not to stop would have been thought very strange.

Now we are hurrying along, cycling through a tree-lined stretch of road with more cottages on our left and fields on our right. In one of these little houses lives a woman with a huge goiter that swells between her face and her chest. The sight of her is both fascinating and frightening to a child, yet Mrs. Sweeney herself is the most cheerful and friendly of women. She laughs a great deal and always waves as we pass. I am both attracted and repelled, a mixture of childish feelings that I suspect this kind and perceptive woman saw quite clearly and understood.

Further down the hill is Tiernan's coal shop, a fascinating place. Mr. Tiernan and his sons sell coal to the surrounding farmers, so beside the house there is a gleaming mountain of what is called sea-coal, the hard, fierce-burning kind found in the local coalfields—in those days called collieries. Because of the coal dust everything about the Tiernans seems black—their driveway, the walls of their house, their goats and sheep, their dogs, even the family members themselves all seem to partake of this veneer of blackness. Mr. Tiernan shouts out a greeting as we pass, and because of his coal-stained face, his lips and gums seem blood red and his teeth gleaming white.

The hill slopes down more steeply as we ride down by the very large police station—a relic of the violence of the earlier part of the century—and then down to the main street. All shops are closed for Sunday, even the public houses (or pubs). But everyone knows that only the front entrances are closed; the back doors provide a welcome for all. On we go into the central square of the town, down its deserted length, then a push on the pedals as the road rises over the small stone bridge across the river. There in front of us, through a shadowed, tree-lined avenue, we see the churchyard gate, the bell ringing loudly and so insistently at this stage that we expect any peal to be its last. But we also know that time in the Ireland of those days is very relative. Service at eleven means service "sometime around eleven," or whenever the rector gets back from whatever other little church he has been to before Saint Mary's.

The sound of the bicycle tires changes as we swing onto the graveled driveway. The dark, tall yew trees glide past us one by one. When we alight in front of the church door, since there is time we go over for a moment to check the flowers on my grandmother's grave. When my grandfather goes with us he always comes to the grave and stands there for a moment before going into the church for the service.

Outside the church door, since the bell is still ringing, there is a gathering of men. The women always go into church, but the men, young and old, stay outside as if by some longstanding but unstated custom. They speak of the things that are going on, farm matters, government things, local events. Their conversations continue until the very last tolling of the bell, when they all troop in and take their seats.

The country churches of the Church of Ireland are to this day simpler and starker than their English counterparts. On this Sunday morning before the Second World War there is no cross on the altar to be a focus for the eye or the mind. There are no candles, though there are flowers behind the bare altar. This starkness is in absolute contrast to the baroque elaboration of the surrounding world of folk Catholicism. The Eucharist, always called the Holy Communion, is celebrated here once a month as the main liturgical act of the day, and the routine of Morning Prayer is in direct and intentional contrast to the frequency and centrality of the Mass in that other world.

This Church of Ireland congregation sees itself as a community of rationality in a vast sea of superstition and emotion, a community of a sacred word read and proclaimed as distinct from a sacramental mystery enacted and celebrated. Even when the Holy Communion is celebrated here at Saint Mary's, it is done with the celebrant standing at the north end of the Holy Table. At no time is he to turn his back on the people, because to do so is to take up the position—and therefore by implication the authoritative role—of the priest in the nearby Roman Catholic church. Needless to say, none of this was known to me as a child, but it would soon be communicated to me in boarding school.

The canon enters from the tiny vestry quickly. He moves with a swift, gliding walk to the prayer desk, turns to us, and announces the opening hymn. He is a tall, thin, austere man, made more so by the contrasting black and white of his preaching scarf, surplice, and cassock. He has been rector of this parish with its three churches for a number of years. At this stage the fashion of the Church of Ireland is still to-

ward long incumbencies. His person and his role are
the focus of deep and unquestioning respect, which
has less to do with who he is than with what he is—
the rector. If his generation of Irish clergy were alive
today they would simply not comprehend the fragile
and nervous relationship now common between
priest and people in parish life, so dependent on per-
sonality and on such things as ever-new parish pro-
gramming and communication skills. On this Sunday
morning in the 1930s the presence of this congregation is not in the least dependent on these things. We
are here because to do so is an utterly taken-for-
granted strand in the tapestry of our lives. Not to be
here would be to stand outside the life of the community. Not to be here would be to break the solidarity of the tribe.

The small group of wives and daughters who
make up the choir rise together, the organ wheezes
to life, and the service begins. The words of Scripture
are read in a detached way that never seeks to con-
vey meaning. The prayers are offered without any
deviation from a totally familiar page of the prayer
book. No personal intercessions are offered, unless
within the silence of some worshiper's private
prayer. The sermon makes no allowances for the
events of the local scene or the spiritual journeys of
those listening. All of these needs and expectations
are still far in the future. Yet, in spite of all the imper-
sonality of the service, there exists among this gathering an almost absolute loyalty. When the prayer
mentions those who are "absent through age, sickness, or any other infirmity," these are, for the most
part, the only reasons for being absent.

This close-knit Church of Ireland congregation is about something that is both more and less than worship. Its gathering here is not so much an expression of worship as it is one of solidarity—cultural, linguistic, and social. As Church of Ireland people we are protected by the constitution of our newly-formed Irish Free State which has allowed freedom of worship, but deep down we know that this same new state is subject to the needs and demands of what may still be, even at the end of the century and in a vastly changed church and world, the most resilient Roman Catholicism of all, that of Ireland.

The service over, we emerge from the church and disperse. There is very little gathering after the service, since contacts have been made before. The canon, still in his cassock, surplice over his arm, is already exiting by the vestry door for another service in the third small church in the parish. A salutation here and there, a gathering up of hymn books and prayer books to be returned home, a burst of laughter somewhere, goodbyes called out, and we are once again on our bicycles heading down the driveway, under the trees, across the bridge, and into the square. This time we must soon dismount and begin the walk up the steep hill that takes us out of the town and onto the road to Donaguile and the farm. By now the streets are deserted: the last Mass is over for our neighbors, and the midday meal is being prepared in the little houses. We walk almost alone as a family, climbing the slope of the valley to the farm. We are outside the rhythms of the majority, outside the ranks of that other great tribe. We are Protestants. We are Church of Ireland.

a warm and loving ghetto

I t is a November evening in Cork. Darkness falls early, but the wind and the rain continue. I am afraid because I must take a short but fearful journey, one that I dread, but I have not said anything to my parents about it. I am going through a strange period in my life, a time of change that remains very vivid in my mind, a memory from a world where the sequence of life changed far less than today.

My family has moved from one side of the city to the other after the doctor ordered my father not to walk the steep hills of the area we have always lived in. This move means a different parish church. I find myself in another school, among strange faces, and in another church choir. The parish church of Saint Nicholas is about the same size as my church, Saint Luke's. It stands on a hill at the end of a curving driveway, overlooking what is to me a poorer part of the city.

To get to the entrance of the choir practice room I must go up the hill, around by the front of the church, and along by the much darker far side. My footsteps on the wet gravel echo against the high, moss-covered wall. The trees loom larger as darkness comes, and, worst of all, as I come around the corner of the wall to reach the door I must pass a large half-sunken tomb of some bygone and illustrious Church of Ireland family. The tomb has long since fallen into disrepair; the railings that surround it are rusty, the grass growing above it is long and tangled, and in the ancient iron door there are four small holes that repel and yet fascinate me. If I were to dare to go near and put my eye to one of those holes, what unimaginable horrors would I see?

Twice a week, once for choir practice and once for Sunday Evensong, I must pass this corner. Choir practice is not so bad because it is after school, when dusk is falling under the gray winter clouds but it is not yet night. But on Sunday evening there is no escape. The bus drops me at the churchyard gate. I run up the driveway, pass around by the west door, turn the corner, and look down the side of the church. There at the end is the tomb. I walk forward, fearfully. To reach the door I must approach the dreaded heap of tangled grass, railings, and old stone. At a certain point I make my dash, sliding on the gravel, careening around the last corner, keeping as close as I can to the wall and as far from the tomb as possible. I grasp the circular iron handle of the church hall door and fall breathlessly and gratefully into the lighted corridor.

The Church of Saint Nicholas stands on a hill on the south side of the city, while Saint Luke's stands to the north. These are only two of the nine large Anglican parish churches dotted throughout the city, not to mention an even larger—and genuinely lovely—cathedral. All this to serve something between three and four thousand people. In the city there are also other small communities of faith: a single Methodist congregation, a Presbyterian church, a Baptist meeting hall, and a small Jewish synagogue. There must have existed a small number of people who subscribed to no religious institution or set of beliefs in particular, although this possibility was almost incomprehensible to the Irish mind. The joke that atheists could in those days be asked if they were Protestant atheists or Catholic atheists is quite possibly derived from that long-ago little world!

Every one of those Anglican churches had been built in the traditional Gothic or Romanesque style. Every one had magnificent marble and stone, stained glass, designed flooring, and brass, wooden, and wrought iron furnishings. Most were surrounded by spacious grounds that would usually contain a churchyard or burial ground. Even the least significant of these churches would today be treasured in any diocese, and in fact many dioceses would be glad to have any of them as their cathedral.

One might ask an obvious question about the burden of what we today would call real estate. The fact is that it had all been built long before the republic had come into being, at a time when Ireland was governed from Westminster and many English families were still in Ireland. While the churches' upkeep—to the degree that they were kept up—was heavy, it was made possible by that saving element in the life of most churches of the older world, endowments. These endowments in the Church of Ireland had been deeply damaged by the disestablishment of the church in the late nineteenth

century, and by the time I was growing up the main-
stay of the church was the donations of parishioners.
Once a year the offerings of every parishioner were
listed and published, and I don't recall that there was
any embarrassment about this. As with so many
things in that time, it was simply the way things
were done.

Although the custom was already dying out in the
cities, in almost every rural parish there would be the
family who lived in "the big house" or on "the estate." Sometimes in an urban parish there would be a
few of these families, living on the outskirts of the
city. These families were affluent, though sometimes
their affluence was one of appearance rather than ac-
tuality. For the most part, their wealth was inherited
and was no longer increasing. Great tracts of land
owned by these formerly wealthy families were by
then gradually beginning to be sold off in order to
keep up a certain way of life. Many of these people
depended on British civil service or army pensions;
they were in fact the last vestiges of what for a long
time was called "the ascendancy." Many of these Anglo-Irish saw it as their inherited duty to be generous
to "their" church.

In the Church of Ireland of those days, the diocese
was a family to a degree that is unknown today in all
but the smallest dioceses. As I have mentioned, in
some ways, both for good and ill, the Church of Ireland was a kind of ghetto that saw itself as a community apart. Certain consequences flowed from this, not
least the cohesiveness of the parish church as a home.
Far more than simply a place for worship, the parish
church was the center of social life for its families.

I realize now that the Church of Ireland parish in my childhood served exactly the same needs as thousands of ethnic parishes in the New World. It was the ocean liner blazing with light in a surrounding dark sea, a refuge in a strange and rather threatening world. For the same reason that every American Roman Catholic parish had its attached parochial school, so did the Church of Ireland. These schools were not so much about education as about the preservation of identity. The same need produced Church of Ireland sports clubs, social clubs, and dances. In a society where government social programs were still sparse, the church had its support systems for its own people. Every diocese had its Church of Ireland Orphans Society; Church of Ireland schools looked to Church of Ireland employers for jobs for their graduates. The truth is that many employers exploited this dependence by offering low salaries and few benefits, knowing that the possibility of employment in the surrounding culture was unlikely, to say the least.

I earned my first income when I was seven. I had been a choirboy for a month and I was enjoying it. I still had not received my own cassock, but that would come eventually; for now, the important thing was that this was the day we were to receive our monthly choir pay. You cannot imagine the intoxication of the pleasure this brought to us, who lived in a society where a child had very few—if any—sources of earned pocket-money. Choir pay was something deeply envied by other boys our age.

We lined up as Mr. Garrett, the choirmaster, fiddled with a bag of change on the piano. With slow and maddening precision, he stacked the coins in little piles and then took a list of our names, which he proceeded to check very carefully. As he called out each name, each boy stepped forward. Mr. Garrett then pronounced the number of times, if any, the boy had been absent and the amount being paid to him before handing him the money.

Since I was the youngest and the most recent arrival, I had no expectation of getting anything—although that is not to say I was not desperately consumed with desire! Suddenly my name was called. The universe swam around me. I rushed forward to hear Mr. Garrett intone, "One shilling and six pence." In all my short life I had never possessed this princely sum. Vast plans formed in my head as I went from the choirmaster's presence.

In those days it was possible to buy very small quarter-pound boxes of Black Magic chocolates. I went into the local store and bought one for my mother, which cost half of my fortune. She has never forgotten that gift of such extravagance, and we have had many a laugh about it since. I don't remember what I did with the other half; I probably frittered it away on this and that during the long weeks that remained until the next payday. But to this day, the words "Black Magic" evoke the feelings of heady excitement of that never-to-be-forgotten Wednesday afternoon.

the isles of the blessed

When you stand on the edge of the Cliffs of Moher in County Clare, facing out into the Atlantic, you are standing on a wall of granite eight hundred feet high. This is the edge of Europe. Far below you the ocean heaves itself against the black gleaming rock, leaving a thin line of white foam endlessly twisting and writhing. About your head gulls wheel, punctuating their long graceful sweeps by their harsh screaming. Almost always a wind is blowing, and more often than not it carries some rain.

Five hundred years ago this was the edge of the western world. I suspect that a thousand years ago it was regarded as the edge of the universe. Just as today's astronomers look out beyond the galaxy to the nearest stars, so human eyes looked out from these western ramparts to the various islands that dot the ocean southwest, west, and north of Ireland. These islands, some of them visible only on a clear day, have always had about them a sense of the mysterious. Even when they are inhabited, as are the Aran Islands off the coast of Galway and the Blasket Islands off the coast of Kerry, an air of mystery and romance still clings to them.

Just as the Norsemen located their Valhalla in the western ocean beyond the sunset, the early Irish storytellers told of a faraway land beyond the sea—Hi Breasil, "the isles of the blessed." The stories they told about it became our stories as children, and these stories reveal something of what the spiritual life of a child was like growing up in my generation.

There was once a time, in actual history as well as in myth, when Ireland, like Britain, was covered with vast forests. Moving through the mythic world of these huge forests is a great and mighty race called the Fianna. They are hunters and warriors; to aid them in their hunting they have huge Irish wolfhounds. The leader of this ancient race is Fionn, or Finn, MacCool, the popular hero of the Gaelic-speaking Irish. Finn has a son whose name is Oisin (pronounced "U-sheen") and who is a poet or bard. In this placing of a poet among the warriors, we catch sight of an ideal that runs through much Celtic myth and history.

One day a beautiful woman on a white horse rides toward the Fianna. She tells them that her name is Niambh Cinn Oir ("Neeve Kang Ore"), or "Neave of the Golden Hair." She tells them that she is the daughter of the king who rules over the islands in the western sea, "the isles of the blessed." Then she issues an invitation, asking Oisin to return with her to her father's palace for a three-day visit, after which he will be free to return. With Finn's reluctant permission, his son leaps up behind Niambh on the great horse and they ride westward like the wind. In some accounts, they ride through the air. At the palace Oisin experiences luxuries and wonders beyond his imagining; the three days and nights fly by. After they are over he longs to return home. Permission is given, but a condition is set. Oisin can take the white horse and go alone, but if he wishes to return to this kingdom in the western isles, he must on no account touch the soil of Ireland.

Oisin returns to his native country and is appalled at what he finds. The great forests are no more; they have become mere woods and groves. Neither his father Finn nor any of the warriors of the Fianna are anywhere to be found. From those of whom he enquires he learns with increasing dread that even their memory has been dimmed by time. The people of this new, unfamiliar Ireland are pathetically weak and small in stature. One day he learns the truth, that no less than three hundred years have gone by since he left, and that he himself and everything he knows is now the stuff of myth and memory.

Bereft of all hope and comfort, Oisin wanders the length and breadth of Ireland, refusing to accept what he has been told. One day he comes across three men who are trying to lift a large stone and who ask him for help. He bends down contemptuously to lift it for them but his stirrup breaks and he comes crashing to the ground. His great horse rears and screams, leaps into the air, and disappears toward the west. On the ground, to the horror of the three watchers, is a withered old man who cannot even stand. The three men lift the fallen giant and take him to a Christian saint who lives nearby and who listens to the old man's story. The saint then tells Oisin of another giant, one who was taken by death and carried away for three timeless days and who returned from the dead. Baptism is offered, and Oisin accepts this new religion just before he dies.

It is difficult as an adult to say how and why this story gripped my mind as a child. To this day, I am always deeply intrigued and moved by any stories involving a journey in time, particularly of a time traveler who has been lost and isolated in another era. There is of course the vividness of this story's images, the heroic quality of its characters, the endless forests, the great hounds and horse, the beautiful woman, the magic islands shimmering in the ocean. However, I think the power of this story for a child lies in some things that will always be the fears of childhood: exile from home, loss of one's family, mystery, perhaps even terror of the helplessness of extreme old age.

There is another story I remember being told as a child. It comes from the loughs and lakes and inlets of the ocean you find all over Ireland, fierce tidal reaches where on dark winter days black water carries white horses of foam on its crests. This story also comes from the narrow channel between Ireland and Scotland; most often these stretches of water are stormy and dangerous, swept by wind and rain. From such a harsh world comes the story of the children of Lir.

Lir was a king in Ireland, kind and good and wise. He and his wife had four beautiful children, three sons and a daughter named Fionnuala. One day their mother, whom the king loved very much, died. The king was desolate but, as time went by, it became obvious that his children needed a mother and his people needed a queen, so he married again. But the popularity of the children and the legendary beauty and goodness of Fionnuala deeply enraged the new queen. Nobody suspected that she had an ancient and evil power to change her own shape and that of others. One day she took the four children to a lake and encouraged them to play in the water. As soon as they were in the water the queen shrieked out the ancient spell, and suddenly the children became four great swans. The children implored their stepmother to give them back their human shapes. She refused, swore the servants with her to secrecy, and left, but not before she had put a further curse on the swans. For nine hundred years they would roam the seas of Ireland, three hundred years on each of three seas and lakes.

As time went by the four swans became known all over Ireland. It seemed as if the female swan carried and led the other three, as Fionnuala had done with her human brothers. Their singing became famous, and because people believed that their song had healing power they were often sought out. Century after century went by, season followed season, storm and calm, rain and sunshine. The swans lived on from generation to generation until the nine hundred years were over.

Knowing that the time was at hand, the great birds flew first to the remembered home of their father. All that remained was a ruin. Once again they rose into the air and flew west to the island of Inishglora in County Mayo, where, it is said, the swans sang so sweetly that all the birds of Ireland came to listen. As they sang, a bell began to toll for matins, the bell of the Christian saint Caemhoch. As the bell rang, it lifted the ancient curse and the swans changed into four very old human beings. The saint offered to baptize them, and as the water touched their withered bodies they died, but for a moment their souls appeared as they once were—young, strong, and beautiful. Thus the children of Lir entered heaven.

It is important to realize that neither of these stories of the islands and the surrounding seas would have been told as a sad story. To the generations of listeners, both Oisin and the children of Lir were given the greatest gifts of all, the gift of baptism as the door into the community of faith and the gift of extreme unction as the door to eternal life.

But such understandings would be for the adults—pious Catholic adults at that. To a child, the stories were powerful for very different reasons. Once again, to capture their power for a child, I have to go back in time—or perhaps it is more a going down into oneself. More than anything else, I think there is in these tales a powerful, haunting "northern-ness." Certainly it was this quality in such myths that spoke to two young writers a generation ahead of mine, C. S. Lewis and J. R. R. Tolkien. So far as I can define, the power of such stories lies in the exile of children from home, the utter loneliness of the landscape, lakes surrounded by impenetrable forests, rocking storm-tossed coastlines, and, perhaps above all, the terror of coming home to find that home is lost in an unattainable past time.

One of my own dreams, dreamed soon after emigrating to Canada, echoes these themes. I dreamed that I was standing by the low wall beside our parish

church in Cork. I was looking down the hill to where
our old home stood. I began to walk up the little gar-
den path. Since I knew where the family key was
hidden, I found it and placed it in the lock. I opened
the door, expecting to see the familiar hall stand with
its coats and hats and umbrellas. But the door
opened on nothing, just a dark void. The dream was
over, and I woke to a feeling of intense desolation. I
realize now it was a dream of crossing over from a
past chapter of life, a dream of learning what we all
must learn, that one can never go home again. I had
taken my place beside Oisin and the children of Lir.

oLɔ goɔs, new faith

*t*he truth is that all of us, Protestant and Catholic alike, were children of an island from which the gods have never really been banished. The legendary Saint Patrick may well have banished the snakes, as the old stories have it—whatever reality of change in tribal custom that vivid myth may hide—but he did not so much banish the old gods as lure them into another pantheon and another faith.

The evidence of this was all around for us to see. We knew of the buildings on their holy island in Lough Derg, a place of constant pilgrimage and retreat to this day. We had the annual climb up the mountain of Croagh Patrick in the western reaches of Connaught, with thousands of barefooted pilgrims bleeding their sins, real and imagined, into the jagged slate-like stones of the pathway that winds upward toward the summit, and the celebration of Mass in the cold, rainy dawn. We had the grottoes at country churchyards, at crossroads, or in river valleys, each with its white, marble-faced statue of the Virgin or of some local saint. These statues would peer ghostlike at us in the evening as we passed on a country road, and as we passed, our hands would instinctively make the sign of the cross. All these places were marked with the same sign of the Christian cross, but they were also rooted in levels of earth and time where far older tales were told and the names of not-forgotten older gods were quietly spoken.

Even in our education, many links between ancient religion and new faith were forged. Because my particular generation was the first of a new fledgling republic, born into bloody rebellion and civil war in 1923, it was thought desirable that we should be given a sense of our own long past as distinct from the then-dominant history of England. A newly created publishing industry saw to it that we were given rich images of Ireland's past. Poetry, saga, legend, story—all lay before us in rich profusion. Again and again these stories would link our pagan past with the coming of the Christian era. We would learn of Laoghaire ("Leary"), High King of Ireland, who was seated one day on his throne at Tara when suddenly a great darkness swept over the palace and the surrounding world. In terror the king sent for his druids to explain this coming of night when it should be afternoon. His druids informed him that this same darkness was sweeping over the whole world because another high king had just died in a faraway land on a cross that was also mysteriously a throne.

Such were the vivid links that were made for us children between pagan and Christian faith. All this gave a unity to religious experience in Ireland, despite the great divisions at the institutional level. Irish Anglicanism might know itself to be part of a great communion bearing that name, but we would rarely if ever hear the actual word "Anglican" used to describe our church. To do so would too easily allow us to be dismissed as English and therefore foreign. The Church of Ireland might have petitions in its prayer book for English monarchs, but its roots also lay in an ancient Celtic past far older than the Reformation. The first bishops of the Irish church may well have been nothing more than tribal chieftains consecrated by Patrick so that whole tribes would come for baptism, but they were still bishops in Ireland soon after the Roman legions had retreated from Hadrian's Wall and had left Britain to the mercy of its next wave of invaders. My generation was taught with much pride that the island of Iona might well lie within a gull's cry of the Scottish coast, but it might never have been heard of were it not for the stormy genius of an Irish monk named Colmcille, or Columba, to give him his Latin name. Through the work of the shadowy giant remembered only as Patricius (Patrick—the Noble One), we were sure that our Irish church sent its roots back into Gaul, further southeast into Rome, and beyond even Rome itself to Jerusalem and Bethlehem.

The predominantly rural forms of ministry in the church in which I grew up moved to the cycles of the seasons and the earth. The absence of cities, factories, and industry made possible a simplicity in both society and in daily life, and therefore a rich pastoral commitment between priest and people. All of these things made the Church of Ireland a church and a faith that, when seen through English eyes, prompted reactions ranging from amused curiosity through puzzled envy to friendly bafflement.

This is the story of Patrick as I remember it from the time I first heard it. In the early hours of Holy Monday in the year 433, gray clouds lumbered eastward before a wind sweeping in from the Atlantic and across the island. A small group of monks embarked from the stony beach that edged the western side of Strangford Lough. Not a word was spoken, as if in deference to the obvious sorrow of their leader, Patrick. Behind them a thin column of smoke lifted and was taken by the wind.

A few hours before they had stood and watched the burning house, listening to the screams of Milchu from within, who had chosen self-immolation rather than face these strangers led by the boy, now a bishop of the church, whom he had once beaten as his slave. All through the long and dangerous voyage from France, Patrick had looked forward to speaking with his old master of the Christ he had found. Instead, Milchu had chosen to die by his own hand, offering himself to the old gods rather than risk an encounter with an emissary of the new. Milchu's death freed Patrick of an obligation, and he was now free to move toward the center of pagan power in the island. They would go directly to the kingdom of Tara, which lay seventy miles to the south. Patrick and his monks would sail down the coast and then try to sail upriver through the endless forest that covered the island. Patrick knew that they would recognize Tara by its elevation above the forest and by the royal acropolis that crowned it.

To edu

They planned to reach the religious and political center of the island by the eve of Easter. Patrick knew that the very word Easter was still unknown in the island. All around them far more ancient gods possessed the innumerable groves and high places. But Patrick remembered the years he had spent here as a boy, captured in a raid on the coast of Britain and sent to mind sheep on the slopes of Mount Slemish in County Antrim. He knew that the druid priests of the old gods venerated fire as a symbol; many a time he had watched the flames leap into the night from the surrounding hills as the priests celebrated the rhythms of the seasons.

They slid down the lough and headed for the open sea. The voyage south, all the way within sight of the shore, was stormy but uneventful. At night they went ashore to sleep. Once, far out to sea, they saw a sail that might mean danger, for now that the Roman legions were retreating piracy was becoming more common. On the third day they rounded the headland, glided into the mouth of the River Boyne, and went ashore. It was Maundy Thursday. That evening they shared bread and wine before the evening meal, and early in the morning they set out along the green bank of the river. All day they walked, resting only when necessary, until toward evening they came to Rossnaree, the burial place of the kings of Ireland. Patrick knew now that they were near Tara. They prepared for the night.

Patrick had planned carefully for Saturday. A nearby hilltop was selected, and he climbed it himself to see whether the palace could be seen. Then for hours the company of monks cut branches and piled them high. At dusk they began the Easter liturgy, their voices rising and falling on the breeze. Patrick glanced again and again to the southwest, for he knew that that night was the celebration of the spring equinox in the druidic cycle of time. He knew also that the high king would have issued an order for the sacred fire to be set ablaze on this night, and that under pain of death no other fire was to be lit. The moment a monk put a torch to the wood piled on this hilltop where they stood, there would be no going back.

Suddenly a distant flame broke the gathering darkness. At Patrick's signal the torch was lit. They waited a moment for the wood to catch, and then with a roar it blazed into the sky. Patrick dressed himself in his bishop's garment, and one of the monks carried the large wooden cross they had brought with them. They left the ring of warmth and light around the fire, moved down the hillside into the trees, and set out toward their confrontation with the high king, his warrior court, and his druids. One age was about to end and another to begin.

To tell that story again more than half a century after I first had it told to me makes me realize what radical changes have come to Christian faith in the intervening years. When that story was told to us there was no question as to who was hero and who was villain, no middle ground between new Christian and ancient druid. Not a single thought was given to the possibility that the millennia-long wisdom of the druids might have something to give to the new faith. Accommodation with their traditions was inconceivable: conquest was the only way. The old faith had to die so that the new faith could be born.

By the end of the twentieth century we have a Christianity so unsure of itself, so apologetic for its every past action, so eager to assign worth to every spirituality other than itself, that we cannot help but wonder sometimes if it is capable of the harsh wilderness journey that it is now called to as its third millennium approaches.

I am in no sense calling for new conquest and a revived triumphalism. But we need to find a stance somewhere between that of conquest and one of abject loss of confidence. It seems to me that for these coming years we need to tell again the stories of our past, particularly those centuries when a great shadow had fallen and all things Christian were driven to the edge of the world. We need to know the stories of those immensely courageous and creative men and women who kindled the fires of Easter in the darkness of their time, and tended its flame until the light came again and a new day dawned.

the island at the end of the world

I was still a child when I first heard of the voyage of Saint Columba to the island of Iona, crossing one of the most treacherous stretches of the eastern north Atlantic and braving the brutal winds of the north channel between Ireland and Scotland. He and his companions made the journey in a *curragh*, a large black boat with long heavy oars. The way in which the story was first told to me says a great deal about the particular way that legends of Irish heroism were communicated to my generation of children.

In 1938, when I was ten years old, the Irish Free State (as it first called itself) was still only fifteen years old. Its life was full of an intense determination to become truly Irish. Everything English, while not entirely rejected—that was simply not possible as a cultural or political reality—was to take second place to things Irish. The Irish language was to be revived from its near death in the late seventeenth century, Irish magazines would be created, Irish plays written. In a word, an Irish world would be formed in which we, the new generation, would grow, find cultural riches, and enter into dialogue with the world beyond the shores of our small island home.

The result of this was the mining of our past history for heroes and heroines like Patrick, Columba, and Brigid. Our schoolbooks were full of the stories of men and women whose exploits were enacted in every century. Added to this was the fact that church life was so strong in the Ireland of those days that there was intense concentration on the Christian past. Consequently, our lives became wrapped up in the saints of the Christian story.

Within the ranks of these figures there was another common factor, that of travel. Irish saints were nothing if not peripatetic: they set out on journeys and voyages at the drop of a hat! I realize now that for those of us growing up in the 1930s, the heavy wooden *curraghs* that took Columba and his monks to Iona or carried Brendan and his companions across the Atlantic were to us what the covered wagons of the early settlers are to American children, or the sailing ships of the early Elizabethan explorers to English children. In all of these narratives, religious faith, exploration, discovery, adventure, and freedom combined to inspire and energize a particular generation.

Irish life has always mingled the poet and the warrior in its concept of the ideal, with both good and bad consequences. One of these consequences is that great literary creativity and considerable violence very often exist side by side. One of Ireland's greatest saints was no exception. His name, Columba, is a later Latin form of Colmcille. Just as *columba* means "dove" in Latin, so *colmcille* means "the dove of the church" in Gaelic. Both names are ironic, for very good reason.

Born in the harsh northern reaches of the Inishowen peninsula in northern Donegal, Columba was rich, imperious, volatile. Everything he did was done with passion. His natural pride found the demands of Christian humility very hard, while a natural instinct for vengeance found the church's demands for forgiveness impossible.

A crisis came about when Columba borrowed a book from another monastery; in those days, books were almost unobtainable and therefore priceless. Columba later returned the book, but only after he had had it copied by hand, and a demand was made for the copy as well as for the original. The case went as far as the court of the high king in Tara, whose verdict went against Columba. In the words of the king, "To every cow her calf, to every book its copy."

A resentful Columba returned the copy, but then gathered the men of his monastery together for battle, which was quite common for the great monastic communities of the time. Most of these religious orders were merely ancient tribal units made Christian by mass baptisms. The result of Columba's battle was an appalling loss of life. For Columba himself the event was traumatic and his reaction typical—passionate rage was followed by passionate remorse. Then he made a life-changing decision: he would leave Ireland forever and give the rest of his life to Christian evangelism. Being the kind of man he was, Columba had no difficulty in getting others to follow him. The great black *curragh* was built, supplies were placed aboard, and they set out for the open sea. It was the year 563. Columba was forty-two years old.

Two weeks later the coastline of Inishowen had dropped away into the mists and the spray. They had moved down the Foyle, checking the seams of the skins along the side of the boat, testing the leather sail. As he took his turn at the oar, Columba smiled as he realized how much he had changed. Once he would have ordered the monks to row, but now he sat at the great oar himself, feeling the rough wood making his buttocks raw and the sea tearing at the muscles of leg and arm, forcing him to bend before the power of MacNannan Mac Lir, ancient god of the sea, now conquered by the Christ who could still a storm. Columba was conscious of no fear. In a dream he had seen an island and a welcoming harbor.

And indeed the wind did take them first to a place of welcome and warmth. The mainland colony of Dalriada in Scotland offered them hospitality, allowing them to rest and gather their strength. From there they headed out to sea again, their voices joining with those on the beach singing psalms until they were out of sight and hearing.

Hours later they saw the island of Iona. At first they thought it was a mere promontory of the mainland, but as they came nearer they saw a stretch of water about a mile wide separated island from mainland. The monks pulled steadily in, carefully avoiding the rocks. Columba went ashore and crossed the field above the beach, heading for the highest point. For a long time he stood facing south. As penance for his great sin he had sworn that he would never again dwell in a place from which he could see Ireland.

Finally he turned and waved. Gladly the monks began to pull the heavy boat up on the beach. Columba gathered them in a circle huddled against the wind and gave thanks for the voyage and for the safe harbor. His voice rose and fell, and his monks could hear all the hope and plans and resolutions pour from him in a flood of lyricism that had earned him the title of Ollamh, or chief poet, in the world they had left. On this lonely windswept island there came together all the richness of language and imagination of a thousand pagan generations fused with the boundless treasury of spirituality found in the young Christ rising to bring back light to a darkened world.

Then Columba's voice fell silent. The sounds of the sea and the wind and the crying of seabirds swept over them, reminding them of their human needs for shelter and food. They set about emptying the boat. A few of them went to select a site that might afford them shelter. The island as yet had no name, so they referred to it merely by the word "island," which in their language was *ioua*. Centuries later a monk, probably weary as he copied a manuscript that told the story of Columba, would make a tiny error and the word would instead become "iona." By then, a prophecy would have been fulfilled that was implicit in a response made by Columba on the day of their landing. One of the monks had remarked that the island was small. Columba turned to him and said, "Yes, but it shall yet be mighty."

In his wildest imagination Columba could not have envisaged the truth of his response. In a very few years he would be sitting at the refectory table listening to a report from one of his young monks named Ninian. The younger man had just returned from a dangerous foray through the lowlands of the mainland inhabited by the fierce and pagan Picts. He was eager to evangelize them. All he needed was Columba's assent. It was given, and a new chapter of Christian history began.

From those lowlands the light and energy of the Iona community would turn south into Northumbria and east to the sea and the small island of Lindisfarne. From there monks would eventually venture across the sometimes inhospitable and vicious North Sea. They would in time enter the river estuaries of the Rhine and the Seine. In various places two or three of them would build their huts and plant a first crop. Gradually they would become part of the life of a neighboring tribe or village. At first the discipline and simplicity of their lives would excite curiosity. Sometimes it would also excite resentment and enmity, resulting in the martyrdom of some of the monks. But gradually the enthusiasm and attractiveness of their faith would begin to draw converts.

A succeeding generation of monks ventured among the white peaks of the Alps, then south into northern Italy and east on the flow of the Danube. Slowly the huts became larger, until the monasteries began to rise, bearing names such as Gall and Columbanus. But wherever the lights of the new monasteries shone in the forests and valleys of Europe, they would all look back to the tiny island of Iona as their spiritual birthplace, the source of the gospel now returning to western Europe and preparing to push back the darkness that had fallen three centuries earlier.

a very gallant gentleman

t takes something very special in a liturgy to impress a choirboy. Such an event occurred in my last year in the choir. The archdeacon, quite elderly and increasingly feeble—but no less feared and respected as an authority about everything—stepped up to the altar to celebrate the Eucharist. He reached out to support himself on the Holy Table (as custom would have called it there at that time). Suddenly he suffered a seizure of some kind and fell backward. All around him was a floor of solid marble slabs and steps. In the split second between the archdeacon's tottering backward and his actually hitting the floor, the curate hurled himself full-length across the sanctuary in a perfectly executed rugby football tackle, cushioning the older man's fall.

It was all over in a moment. Anyone deep in the pages of the prayer book would have missed it. But not us choirboys, who never looked at any page unless it was directly and absolutely necessary for our required singing. We saw every millisecond of the delicious melodrama. The new curate rocketed to dizzying heights in our admiration.

The next day the tale was all around the schoolyard. The curate himself even used the event in a talk to us after choir practice later that week. To recall that moment and how widely it became known reminds me of the extent to which our community was a tightly-knit one, as well as the extent to which almost all of the activities of our lives were based within the life of the church, most of them even within the church buildings themselves.

It is 1940. Sunday school is at 9:30 a.m. each week. The classes are small because we are a small community. In my circle there are six to eight boys. Eventually, four of us in this tiny circle will be ordained as priests. For now we are typically restless, inattentive pre-teen boys. Our attention is fleeting, grasped only by either an Old Testament story of sufficient barbarism to appeal to our bloodthirsty minds, or, even better, one hinting of the as yet largely unexplored country of sexuality.

At 10:30 we leave this class and rush to a short choir practice before choral Morning Prayer at eleven. After the service we thunder down the winding, narrow staircase from the vestry and line up outside the choir room. The choirmaster walks up and down in front of us, giving his sometimes very candid opinion of our singing and of our behavior. His comments ended, he barks the command to pray, and our heads flop forward while the prayer is offered in a sing-song voice. In spite of all the distractions, the prayer has remained with me for a lifetime:

> Grant, O Lord, that what we have said and sung
> with our lips we may believe in our hearts, and

that what we believe in our hearts we may practice
in our lives, through Jesus Christ, our Lord.

We chorus a hearty "Amen" and rush for the cupboards, tearing off Eton collars, ruffs, surplices, and
cassocks, pitching them onto shiny brass hooks used
by generations before us. We then tramp noisily and
boisterously into the church grounds, scattering hun-
grily for our houses.

At three in the afternoon many of us will meet
again for a half-hour children's service. Released
from that, we are free until six, when we must head
back for choir practice followed by Evensong at
seven. After that some of us will head off to a nearby
Presbyterian church for a Bible class run by the Boys'
Brigade. At that class one evening, in the course of
some Bible study whose chapter and verse is now
gone, the leader said to us, "Always remember that
you were put on earth to do something for God that
nobody else can do in quite the same way." It is
strange how certain moments remain in my memory,
when everything that came before and after them is
completely lost. Why is that single sentence remembered forever? God knows.

Such was the sequence of our lives in those years
before I turned thirteen. Then everything changed.
Like most of my friends, I was now bound for boarding school. Midleton College sent its roots back into
the late seventeenth century. Its motto—*Spartan Nac-
tus Es, Hanc Exorna*—loosely translated, means "You
were born a Spartan and you will live up to it." So
we did! It was a very spartan place indeed. When I
took my grown-up family to see it many years later,

they were appalled at the severe furniture and decor, the hard seats of the so-called library, the monastically simple beds, the stairs smoothed and gnarled by generations of pounding boots and shoes, the dark caverns where one showered after games. Ironically, I myself thought the place had softened and mellowed considerably since my time! I first entered its gates and walked up the driveway about seven in the evening of September 9, 1941, homesick and fearful but determined not to betray these feelings. This place would be my home, except during the fleeting intervals of school holidays, for four years.

At Midleton such things as Sunday school, children's service, church choir, and Bible class would become things of the past, their place taken by another routine. Each Sunday morning, under the watchful eye of the schoolteacher on duty, every boy in the school would line up and march to the village church in a long two-by-two line, juniors in front, seniors behind, everyone in school uniform, everyone present with no exceptions other than genuine sickness. Each Sunday evening exactly one quarter of the school lined up in precisely the same way for Evening Prayer. That meant that each of us went to Evening Prayer once a month, give or take, since I can't remember what happened on the few fifth Sundays in the month!

Each morning of the week the school assembled for prayers in the gymnasium. There was a certain medieval grimness to these fifteen minutes. Announcements were read out; during my years the Second World War was raging and the deaths of former schoolboys (usually referred to as Old Boys) on active service would be announced when the sad news would come. Major punishments were also administered for infractions like cheating on an examination or stealing or even breaking something valuable while fighting with another boy. So a public caning was sometimes part of the pattern of worship. I now realize that these events, admittedly rare but even more sobering because of their rarity, were not entirely unlike public burnings at the stake in the context of some appropriate liturgy in earlier centuries.

Each week we sat through two school periods of religious instruction, taught as a regular part of the curriculum. As the springtime of the year approached, so did "The Synod," the short name for the examination set by the Church of Ireland's General Synod for every child in its schools. As this examination approached, more and more time was set aside for Scripture and church doctrine, until just before the examination all other subjects ceased to be taught for at least a week and the whole school day was given over to these subjects. Today this must sound like science fiction! At least in my own case, that immersion in Scripture and church doctrine, an education so totally different from anything in today's schools, gave me an intimacy with the text and world of both the Bible and the prayer book that has stood me in good stead through the years.

Such was the means by which we were inculcated with a great deal of religious information. But a dimension other than information was needed. Fortunately for us, it was provided by the gentle, learned, and sensitive priest who was the rector of the local parish and who prepared us for confirmation.

At this point I am nearly fifteen and have been at boarding school for almost two years. The rhythm of its life has by now become the rhythm of mine; as with many of my generation, I will never again live at home except during school holidays. In a few years I will go from here to university and from there into one of the professions. This pattern is taken absolutely for granted by all concerned—the school, my parents, and myself. Quite simply, it is what young Protestant men did unless some extraordinary circumstance interrupted this sequence.

Confirmation was also an expected part of this pattern. Confirmation classes were not the prerogative of the school; instead, they were the responsibility of the rector of the local parish. He had a very strong link with the school because we sat before him for services every Sunday in the parish church. Now, in this year of our confirmation, we will get to know him more intimately because confirmation classes will take place in his study in the rectory.

The place of our confirmation classes may sound like a mere detail, but to us it meant very much more because from the time that the school term began to its end, we never got to leave. Weekends home were unknown, as were parental visits. To go into someone's home, as distinct from the institutional corridors and dormitories of the school, was something we longed for and looked forward to with an intensity beyond words. For this reason more than for any other, confirmation was anticipated with passion.

Once a week we would go out of the smaller side gate of the grounds and walk the two hundred yards or so to the rectory, a large red brick house on its own gracious grounds. I noticed on the very first Wednesday afternoon that for once we were not lined up for this walk, but were allowed to walk as we wished—alone, with a friend, or in a small group, and we were not under the escort of a senior or a teacher. This in itself was an immense affirmation of our sudden maturity and seniority. If this is what confirmation was to mean, we thought, then let it come with all possible speed!

The rector of the local parish was a gracious and courteous man with a slender, fine-boned face, a quiet voice, a gentle manner. He had silver hair that shone under the light of the standard lamp that stood in his study and warmed our gatherings on those evenings when the daylight began to fade before class was over. Even now in recalling him and those precious hours spent in his home, I can recapture the intense pleasure of those times.

I realize now that it was only the study and the hallway of the rectory that were available to us. We entered the hallway, caps and coats were taken off and duly deposited somewhere, then we turned right into the study. There was a large desk, behind which the rector sat, in the early classes. Later on he tended to sit on the edge of the desk, his legs crossed, his hands grasping one knee. A few of us captured whatever soft chairs were there; others sat on the carpeted floor—a luxury in itself!

In the fashion of those days, there was always a fire burning in the fireplace. On the walls were framed photographs, mainly of groups of stalwart young men, a younger rector somewhere among them, holding oars or cricket bats or tennis racquets against a background of boarding school or university playing fields. Among these photographs was a large one of a very beautiful young woman. It took me a while to realize that this was none other than the friendly and gracious woman who sometimes welcomed us to the rectory! I suspect that this realization was my first inkling of what I would later come to know as the changing face of a maturing love.

Over the fireplace hung a painting of a frozen landscape hidden by flying snow. Almost hidden in darkness is a tent. A few yards outside the tent a figure clad in furs is leaning against the wind, trying to make progress against it. Underneath the painting are the words "A Very Gallant Gentleman." In those days none of us needed to be told what the subject of the painting was. The incident of the self-sacrifice of Captain Titus Oates on the ill-fated Scott expedition to the South Pole was part of our mythology. Oates, who had deliberately walked into the storm to give the other three a chance of making it back to base on the remaining food supply, was often presented to us as a kind of Christ-like figure.

I have no particular recollection of specific things taught us in those confirmation classes. My memory is rather of a rich, eagerly awaited weekly experience. Just being there was everything, quite apart from what went on in the classes. But there is one thing, again an image rather than anything explained, that I recall with absolute clarity. Toward the end of the series of classes, when confirmation itself was very near, the rector leaned back across his desk, opened a drawer, and pulled out a picture. He held it up before us and said, "If you forget everything else I have said to you in these times together, I want you to remember this picture."

It was a replica of an old and once very well-known painting entitled *The Vigil*. The painting showed a knight, complete with armor and a red cross emblazoned on his breast, his helmet and sword laid aside, kneeling before a chapel altar. As the rector held it before us he spoke quietly and simply about being faithful all our lives.

Since that evening of long-ago springtime, succeeding worlds of fashion, culture, and belief have come and gone. So much so that it would now be easy to make that image naïve and simplistic, even— the greatest of all modern sins—politically incorrect! All I can say is that for at least one boy in that study—and I am quite sure there are others—the rector's hope that the image would never be forgotten came true.

the pages of time

I t is a Thursday morning late in the autumn term of 1942. I am now in my second year of boarding school. From where we sit in our tenth-grade classroom we can look out across the front playing field and down the long driveway to the main gates. It is about eleven in the morning and we know the only morning bus from Cork should by now have arrived in the main street of the village.

The arrival of the bus is a matter of great importance to us in this particular grade. Our concern is whether or not a certain passenger is on this bus. The mere thought that he may not be sends a thrill of apprehension through each one of us. Throughout this last period before lunch, a history period, we take every opportunity to glance down the driveway. Since Mr. Smith, our history teacher, is perfectly aware of what is going on, it goes badly for anyone actually caught looking out the window.

Suddenly an invisible signal ripples through the whole room. Someone has seen him. Mr. Sheehy is coming through the gate at the end of the driveway, a small tubby figure in his raincoat and floppy hat, his hands in his pockets, his steps short and quick. Sometimes in inclement weather he arrives drenched; sometimes he is half blown along the length of the driveway, grimly hanging onto his hat. But however he arrives, he is welcome to us beyond measure, and a sigh of relief goes through the class. If he did not arrive to take us for a blessedly long double-period of drawing each Thursday afternoon, we were very likely to have an extra period of mathematics with the headmaster, an experience we all dread because it may involve physical punishment.

Bill Sheehy, as the older boys in the senior grades speak of him (though never to his face), is the art teacher. He is not a full-time member of the staff, so he does not live in. He lives in Cork and comes to the school twice a week to teach drawing. A stocky man with a deep voice and a friendly, chuckling laugh, he never wears a black gown as the other teachers invariably do. In a school of intense and sometimes harsh discipline, his class is an oasis of relaxation and pleasure for us. Looking back now, I suspect that this kind man knew very well what life was like in the school, and he set out to be reassuring and relaxing when he was among us.

As Mr. Sheehy enters the classroom, his physical movements belie his girth and weight. His walk is graceful and his arm and hand movements are beautiful as he draws on the blackboard. First, he asks one of us to go forward and clean the whole blackboard. Then, a trifle ceremoniously, he takes a new, full-length piece of chalk—not for Mr. Sheehy the little stubs of chalk used by the other teachers—and effortlessly draws a rectangle twice as long as it is wide. He pauses, and then at each end of the rectangle he draws a semi-circle. Quickly he adds two longer curves that sweep from one end of the rectangle to the other and joins the first two semi-circles. His hand movements gather speed as each curve is elaborated until we see a wonderfully symmetrical design. Mr. Sheehy then turns, smiles at us, and tells us once again that in this rectangle is the basic design of Celtic art, and with it we can make an endless number of variations if we wish.

Some years later, when I got to university, I remembered Mr. Sheehy and the graceful sweeps of his long chalk. There I learned that what he was doing on those blackboards had been done by artists in the Celtic world for at least a thousand years. The proof lay in a collection of pages bound together sometime in the eighth century and found in the nineteenth century by a farmer in the dry bogland of County Meath.

I am in the eighteenth-century Long Room of the university, its original library. The hall itself is magnificent, long and high. Its upper floor contains two great galleries of leather-bound volumes that flow away into the shadows of a winter afternoon. Here we students sit during the morning or afternoon breaks between lectures, studying for approaching examinations. At this time, in the late 1940s, there is no heating in this building, at least none that is discernible. We sit at tables, wearing overcoats and mufflers. Some of us wear woollen hand muffs without fingers so that we can write. On particularly cold days we can see our own breath rise slowly to join the higher shelves of old volumes.

Halfway down this long gallery there is a low, glass-topped case about the height of the tables around it. From time to time visitors come in very quietly. They go to the glass top, gaze into it, whisper to each other, and depart. Some stay a long time if there is no one else waiting, as there very seldom is. As students we hardly glance in that direction because the contents of the case have become totally familiar to us. Perhaps there is always something of the Philistine about students: they are hard to impress. Within a few yards of us lies one of the treasures of western civilization—the Book of Kells, one of the world's very few illuminated manuscripts from a long-ago Celtic civilization.

Now it is forty years later, and I am bringing my family to this Long Room. All traces of our study tables are gone, for the area is no longer used as a place of study, at least for lowly students. The whole gallery is now splendidly lit to show its architectural glory, and heated to a precise degree that best serves the preservation of the book that lies at its heart. The Book of Kells itself is now placed in a much more elaborate casing that affords it a greater degree of security than it needed in the simpler and more orderly society of the 1940s. And everywhere in the gallery itself, lined up outside the landing at the entrance and down the sweeping curved staircase, is an endless line of summer tourists from all over the world, among them my family.

Slowly we shuffle forward as the line moves. We are halfway up the staircase when an elderly man in a black gown comes out of a nearby door and walks very slowly to the exit. I realize with a shock that I am looking at a faculty member who was striding about in the first exhilaration of tenure when I first came up these stairs to study. Eventually we find ourselves at the glass case. I notice that the whole presentation is much more elaborate and technical than I remember. But there, now set in a pool of light to emphasize its priceless beauty, remains the Book of Kells.

More than a thousand years ago, seated in the frigid wind-blown stone hut of his monastic community, an artist whose name we shall never know bent over the page of vellum, dipped his thin brush into the inks he had so carefully made, and began his incredible self-imposed task of copying the four Gospels. As I look again at the particular page opened on this particular day—each day a different page is turned—I realize with awe how much the word "copying" fails utterly to do justice to this achievement. Actually what scholars have since found out from their study of the Gospels is that the book—which has some pages missing from both the beginning and the end—is the work of a series of monastic artists.

The first artist set out to copy the Gospels in a way never before attempted. Because I have seen many of these pages over the years, and because a magnificent facsimile edition is now available, I know that sometimes the artist will give a whole page to one sentence or to a single word, or even, on occasion, to one enormous blazing capital letter at the beginning of a chapter. To look at any page is first to see the overall designs, shimmering in their different colors, riotous in their profusion. Then, bending down, the eye sees smaller designs within those first seen. Detailed, microscopic images appear next, this third level of design almost hidden from sight. All of this

has been done by a human hand and eye, totally
without any but the simplest tools.

Our son, who was fourteen years old at the time of
our visit, thought the book was "neat." Experience
told me that for him to make any unsolicited expression of appreciation at that age was an indication
that he was indeed aware, however dimly, that he
had been in the presence of something beautiful. Perhaps that awareness of the beauty of Irish art was
part of the pleasure we took in Mr. Sheehy's drawing
classes. He was the first to show us that Irish art had
given the world something priceless. We would later
learn the poetry of Yeats, the plays of John Synge
and George Bernard Shaw, the prose of James Joyce.
But Mr. Sheehy opened a world of discovery for us,
and the sight of that long line of visitors with my son
among them, coming to pay tribute to the beauty of
an Irish work of art, was immensely satisfying to one
who had grown up on that small island.

A more recent moment brought back the Long
Room of Trinity College and the illuminated manuscript under its gleaming metal and plate glass, as I
was moving through the Shrine of the Book in Jerusalem. At the center of that very different but equally
magnificent building, under a vaulted, circular chamber, there is another of the world's priceless posses-
sions: the scroll of the Book of Isaiah. As I stood there
a guide was speaking quietly to a group of Jewish
young people visiting from the United States. It was
obvious that the young guide was herself deeply ap-
preciative of what she was showing. She was wise
enough not to be overlong with her youthful audience. At one stage I heard her say simply but effec-

tively, "We are looking at some of the most powerful and beautiful thoughts in human history."

I had lingered at the scroll because my mind had already been making connections back to the Book of Kells, so I was moved by what she had said. As with the Isaiah scroll, the Book of Kells had remained hidden for centuries. But what I found more significant was what both of these books represented as a contribution to the human story. Both of them had been copied by communities who felt they had been banished to the edge of the world and who believed they were living at a dreadful time in history. In spite of this, both of these scribes, one on the edge of an eastern desert and the other beside a western ocean, had decided that the most worthwhile thing to do in the face of all that was threatened was to copy the most precious words they knew. As I stood by that ancient scroll in Jerusalem and remembered the work of another scribe of ages past, I was quite simply glad that someone in the long tradition that had shaped me had also given a great and sacred gift to the world.

the house on
mountjoy square

O ne day in 1938 I was outside the house playing when a familiar figure rounded the corner at the end of the street, parked his bicycle outside our house, and went in. After a while I was asked to come inside to meet him. In the small parlor his black-clad legs seemed to stretch halfway across the room. His name was Fred Johnston—to me, the Reverend Mr. Johnston—and he had recently arrived as the new curate, just ordained and now in his first parish.

As a choirboy I had seen him and met him before. We boys all liked him because he actually talked to us, and I found it easy to talk to him now. He asked the usual things, such as how was I getting on at school, did I like the choir, what games did I play, and all the questions a kindly adult might ask a ten-year-old boy to make some conversation. But he seemed genuinely interested in me; I instinctively felt he was talking to me because he actually liked me. Finally my mother made a motion that I recognized as a signal to leave as gracefully as any ten-year-old can. I mumbled something about it being nice to see him and slid self-consciously toward the door. As I did so he grinned at me across the room, the kind of grin that made me feel that he and I were somehow friends, and then he said, "Maybe you'll be a clergyman some day."

When I entered the Divinity Hostel at Trinity College in the fall of 1949, Dublin was beginning one of the happiest and most attractive times of its long history. Ireland's neutrality during the Second World War had kept the city immensely alive. Its galleries, antique shops, theaters, and restaurants attracted people from the rest of the British Isles, where many of the cities were still trying to recover from the damage and trauma of wartime. Although tourism as a vast phenomenon was still in the future, the accents of Europe and the United States were beginning to sound in the streets, restaurants, pubs, and particularly in the universities, most of all in Trinity College.

Dublin and Trinity are part and parcel of one another, yet distinctly different. The university is at the absolute heart of the city, and as one leaves the city streets and walks the few yards from College Green through Front Gate and into Front Square, suddenly the noise of traffic is muted, and smooth twentieth-century asphalt gives way to eighteenth-century cobbles. One has stepped back in time to a place where most of the population is clothed in black gowns. Here, in this small world of ease, privilege, and learning, not to mention laughter, foolishness, and periods of excess followed by penury, I would spend much of the next four years. Elsewhere in the city, in a very different area devoid of either ease or privilege, I and some of my fellow students would live.

The area of Dublin north and east of the heart of the city was once defined by George Bernard Shaw as the most noble slum in Europe. Its nobility lies in its magnificent Georgian architecture, but in the 1950s other signs of nobility were few unless they lay hidden in the hearts of the men and women and children who lived in the dark, dilapidated interiors of these once glorious houses. Standing like an island in this sea of misery, the north side of Mountjoy Square had managed to retain some vestiges of its former state. Here two houses had been joined to form the Divinity Hostel of the Church of Ireland. Here and there in the same square other houses likewise defied their surroundings. On the east side of the square stood the Jesuit College harshly immortalized by James Joyce in his novel *Portrait of the Artist as a Young Man*. In its pages one sees a classic example of the contradictory relationship between the Anglo-Irish literary mind and the Roman Catholic Church, each both fascinated and repelled by the other.

Here in the hostel we students lived in community, each of us with his own cubicle, and I emphasize cubicle rather than room. The rooms of these great houses were cavernous enough to serve the lifestyle of affluent and titled Georgians of an earlier age. Their ceilings were fourteen feet high, their windows stretched almost to the floor. But the great fires that had once heated these rooms had long since been extinguished, and the window frames had long ceased to fit as they should. The wooden partitions forming our cubicles reached about two-thirds of the way to the ceiling. When I was a student the Bishop of the Arctic came on a visit to Dublin, stayed at the

Divinity Hostel, and remarked that in all his arctic journeys he had never felt so cold!

The hostel itself had no academic program; it was merely a residence and all lectures were given at the university. Yet the hostel did set out to inculcate in us the beginnings of an ordered worship life. That this was carefully and devotedly carried out was due to the quiet, shy, saintly priest who presided over our lives. Michael Lloyd Ferrar lives in my memory as a mentor for whose life and ministry I give thanks at seasons such as All Saints'. Ferrar was a stern man who knew the material he was dealing with. He was aware of a wider world and a wider spirituality than that of the Irish church, had a great interest in the world of Orthodoxy, and had for a while worked in India. He knew that in the Church of Ireland he had to challenge a general carelessness in matters of liturgy and devotional life, for Irish Christianity has always, for good and for ill, been more passionate than disciplined. To try to temper these inclinations, Ferrar saw to it that we adhered to a strict discipline of liturgical life in the hostel, and various rosters listed the names of those who were down for Matins or for Evensong or for some function in the Eucharist. If these schedules clashed with some personal agenda, it was very difficult to get excused.

Michael Ferrar disliked the superstitions of Irish rural life, especially those rituals and beliefs that were really echoes of a pagan past. One evening I was sitting beside him at the formal evening meal we all shared in the hostel. As warden, he sat at the end of a long table and every evening a different pair of us sat at his right and left hand. This was not a privilege we eagerly sought, because he was not a man for much small talk.

On the evening that I was sitting next to him, as I was passing the salt cellar I accidentally spilled a little, and without a moment's thought I took some of the spilt salt and threw it over my left shoulder. I had always done this—it was how you blinded the devil as he looked over your shoulder and saw that you had brought yourself bad luck by spilling salt. The warden was galvanized into action. He got red in the face, stumbled for words, agitatedly transferred his table napkin from one hand to the other, and proceeded to ask me, "Are you or are you not preparing to be a Christian priest?" Completely taken aback at this explosion of emotion from a usually quiet superior, I stuttered, "Yes, sir!" "Then what do you mean by this display of pagan nonsense?" "I...I...I don't know, sir!" "Then never let me see you do this again. Never. Do you hear?" "Yes, sir!" There was a dead silence along the length of the table until slowly the conversation gathered again. I have never thrown salt over my shoulder since. Mind you, I have been tempted, but I have not succumbed!

An interesting encounter played a continuing part in the life of the hostel, that between ordinands from Northern Ireland and those from the Republic. In the early 1920s, when the country was divided politically, the Church of Ireland insisted on remaining unified. However, its numerical strength lay—and to an even greater extent still does—in the north. The main difference between the north and the south was the fact that the north became industrialized. Belfast in particular developed a large working class which, unlike that of England, remained within the life of the church at least up to the years after the Second World War. The south remained largely rural during this time, with very little industry and therefore much less of an urban working class. What there was of such a class in the south was almost wholly Roman Catholic. The Church of Ireland in the south, whether or not it would have been prepared to admit this, was in fact largely rural except in the Dublin area, and almost wholly middle-class.

From these two worlds we met in the Divinity Hostel. For us southerners, the northern men seemed brash, overconfident, dull, practical, ambitious, and militantly Protestant. To them, we southerners tended to appear as dreamers and poets—rural, impractical, mystical, and—worst of all—possibly soft on Roman Catholicism!

I recall vividly one morning during my student days when I had composed what I thought at that early stage to be a wonderful contribution to Christian hymnody. Clutching my newly-minted verses, I went looking for someone, anyone, to share them with. Most people were long gone to various Saturday events and encounters, but at last I discovered a seminarian from the north who shall remain nameless. It was a warm Saturday in early summer and he was sitting at an open window contemplating the square. I rushed up to him and begged him to listen while I recited my new hymn. He let me finish. There was a pause, and then, with all the crushing superiority of a third-year man to a first-year nonentity, he said rather wearily, "I haven't the slightest idea what you're talking about."

All in all, the Divinity Hostel was a quiet, rather gracious, and simple world. It was also very traditional and, by today's standards, very limited and perhaps ingrown. Yet it did hold out some riches for us from time to time. Distinguished figures would appear in order to attend some conference, to preach at some special event, to do some library research, or perhaps to conduct a retreat. Sometimes, if there was an opportunity, arrangements would be made for the visitors to speak to us about their work and their world. Thus we had rich links from our island church to the rest of the world. We were fortunate because, although we did not yet realize it, the world that had formed us and the Church of Ireland was about to be radically changed everywhere.

At the heart of this simpler world, largely unsaid because it was so naturally assumed, was a conviction that the faith once given to the saints was eternal. Theologians, with their books and their schools of thought, would come and go; both in spite of them and because of them the faith would remain. We ourselves would bring such gifts and abilities that we had, strutting our little time on the vast stage of Christian history. In spite of us as much as because of us, the faith would be passed on, served by our gifts and surviving our failures. It was ironic that though the Church of Ireland took great issue with the Roman Catholic claim expressed in the phrase "the infallibility of the church," the same certainty of the church's inevitable presence within and beyond history lay at its own heart and was communicated to us as priests.

the gateway on college green

assive and grey, its pillars blackened by the grime of a couple of centuries, the Chapel of the Most Holy and Undivided Trinity stands in Front Square at the heart of Trinity College, Dublin. During my years there it housed a form of worship that had not changed perceptibly for generations. Morning Prayer reigned supreme and was celebrated with all the solemnity that an essentially simple office can muster. Readers of lections were led to the lectern. Preachers were led from their seat at the very rear of the long chapel aisle, their progress prefaced by a vast silver mace borne by a college official whose single and perennial facial expression mingled utter detachment and infinite world weariness. We students soon realized that since this unfortunate human being had to be present every Sunday, this demeanor was his carefully constructed survival technique. We realized this because we, too, soon learned that all clergy who were invited to preach in the chapel were overcome by their being invited to stand in this august and historic pulpit. They would then feel it incumbent upon themselves to be as excruciatingly turgid and as obscurely learned as they were capable of being. Among many opening sentences of homilies in that chapel, two take pride of place in my memory.

Resplendent in his doctoral robes, a red gown on a black cassock, the Professor of Mental and Moral Science followed the mace to the pulpit. He was prepared to address us on a text (now long forgotten) that would allow him to give us a dissertation on the nature of time. His opening sentence, presumably calculated to grip our undergraduate minds and bring us to the edge of our seats, went as follows: "My friends, as all of us know, there is a cosmic influence which impinges implacably and imperiously upon the terrestrial." Memory has mercifully erased all that followed.

Yet another Sunday saw the Regius Professor of Divinity following the mace forward as the anthem died away. It was a gray Sunday in January; I recall this fact because the lections were those for Saint Paul's feast day. The Regius bowed our heads for the traditional short ascription before the homily. We all sat down. There was a moment's silence, the text was given. Another pause. Then, into the expectant silence the Regius declaimed, "Saint Paul, I would have you all know, was no reactionary obscurantist." Once again, memory has drawn a veil over the inert body of that sermon.

The Divinity School of Trinity College, where all ordinands for the Church of Ireland were prepared for ordination, was set fully within the life of the university. Because Trinity had been an Elizabethan foundation, the Divinity School was the oldest faculty of the university. Up to the turn of the twentieth century it was not possible to be a fellow of the university unless one was an ordained priest of the Church of Ireland. At the end of my third year of arts I entered the Divinity School, mixing arts and theology that year. The following two years, after I had finished my arts degree, would be theology alone, divided for the most part among Old and New Testament studies, church history, and church doctrine.

Other areas would also be attended to, but in a rather perfunctory way. For instance, very little attention was accorded to the fact that for the rest of our lives we would have the unrelenting responsibility to sound reasonably intelligent and interesting about some aspect of Christian faith every Sunday in the pulpit. The area of homiletics, as in many Anglican institutions to this day, was taken rather for granted. However, in our case we were encouraged to join one of the two debating societies of the university—either the Philosophical Society or the Historical Society—and learn there the art of public speaking, a suggestion that I value to this day.

The area of liturgics was equally vague and haphazard, taught by a local rector who came in twice a week and really did little else than improve our reading skills. What today would be known as pastoral theology was largely unknown as an academic discipline. Looking back from today's vantage point, it seems almost amusing that there took place in my final year what was then a radical departure in the Divinity School curriculum. We were given one lecture each on the psychology of Carl Jung and Sigmund Freud. So extreme was this step that a practicing psychiatrist was imported from London on both occasions. One can easily imagine how limited would be the usefulness of these two fleeting glances of a vast new world that was then opening. However, when one knows the situation of that place and time, one can see that even this step was indeed courageous and farsighted.

In the Ireland of those years immediately following the war, the world of psychology was deeply mistrusted by all Christian traditions, and particularly by the Roman Catholic Church. In 1953, there were three practicing psychologists in the whole country, and one of them was a Methodist minister; in his case, it was his ordained ministry that validated his practice of psychology, while today the reverse might be true. In those days for anyone in Ireland to consult any such practitioner would have been thought eccentric, irresponsible, almost immoral, because it would have been seen as denying the accepted role of the clergy and therefore providing further proof that the person did indeed have terrible things to hide. Thus one can understand the courage it took to introduce this strange foreign world into our theological awareness.

The theological lectures we attended were still called by their medieval name, praelections. We were expected to take continuous and copious notes, just as the students in the year ahead of us had written equally copious notes as they listened to exactly the same lecture, as would those in the year after us. I realize now that we were being given theology as a deposit from the past rather than as something living and dynamic; in this sense, the object of the exercise was to pass on a tradition. Most of those theological lectures were about the centuries already past: the early fathers of the church, the Caroline divines, the controversies of the Reformation and Counter-Reformation. The Regius Professor of the time, a shy, aging bachelor whose specialty was the life and work of Irenaeus—or was it Eusebius?—was wont to say frequently that if something is true it is not new and if new it is not true. That was a sentiment which, in those days, given his considerable authority over our professional futures, we were not inclined to challenge.

Contemporary theological thinking was not unknown to us, however. It was the duty of the Archbishop King's Professor to acquaint us with this, and so we were duly informed in a somewhat detached fashion of the work of certain German theologians. We were told of Dietrich Bonhoeffer, whose name had just become prominent because of his death, Rudolf Bultmann and his work of demythologizing Scripture, and Paul Tillich, who, we were assured, might be comprehensible if he were astute enough to exchange his English translator for some Irish writer who would translate his thoughts into readable English! It would be about at this point that the lecturer would regale us with the statement that theology is created in Germany, corrected in Britain, and corrupted in America. Last, but not least, we were given one lecture on the work of Karl Barth.

I realize now that certain messages were subliminally received in those sessions of long ago. One of these messages was that while it was desirable to know about these people, and to know at least something of what they thought and wrote, it was extremely unlikely that they would ever be anything more than peripheral to our lives and work. For one thing, these people were neither Anglican nor Roman Catholic; therefore, they were of doubtful consequence! And they were all very far away—in Europe or America. It was as if an elective in tropical diseases were to be offered in medical school; such diseases would be rather interesting if you had the time and inclination to study them, but were highly unlikely to turn up in the medical practice of anyone listening!

Once again, certain things are easier to see as one looks back. It would be a mistake to be overcritical of those past methods and efforts. Clerical life differed greatly from the present in the time that we would have available for further study if we wanted it. The simple fact is that parish life was less brutally demanding than it is today. If we wished to carry on further investigation of various theologians, then we could do so without fear of a score of deadlines being missed, or of being absent from yet another planning meeting—that term was unknown—or of one's parishioners assuming that theological study was proof of their priest's laziness and impracticality! While we may be tempted to smile at the thought of one lecture each on Freud, Jung, and Barth, at least it pointed the way ahead if we were inclined to go further, and at least some of us were.

So from the point of view of much of today's seminary training, particularly in North America, the theological education we received in the 1950s might seem haphazard and inadequate. I have mentioned the essentially simple training in liturgy we received, the almost total absence of what we would today call pastoral theology, the very minimal instruction given in homiletics. However, when you understand the point of view of that time and the kind of society we were expected to function in as priests, the picture looks rather different.

The first reason for what from today's vantage point might seem a cavalier attitude to the essentials of a seminary curriculum was that in those days it was taken absolutely for granted that every one of us would go from our ordination to at least one if not two curacies under the supervision of an experienced parish priest. Each of these curacies would last at least two years, sometimes longer, which meant that none of us would be given our own parish for at least four and quite possibly six or seven years after ordination. It was during these years that we would learn how to preach, would learn what it meant to be pastorally wise and responsible, and what it meant to be a good liturgist.

However, the most important difference between our situation and that of today lay in something not as precisely defined but nevertheless of great significance. To a degree difficult if not impossible to experience today, our ministry was exercised in a society where many assumptions could be made that are now no longer possible. We could presume that our ministry would be accepted, understood, and appreciated everywhere we went. It rarely if ever occurred to us that we would find ourselves in a position of having to explain the Christian faith to anyone, at least in a basic, introductory sense. The concept of mission was understood only in terms of leaving the country and going into "the mission field." In those days the mission to Chota Nagpur in India was a particular interest of the Church of Ireland and provided an element of the glamorous and the exotic in our lives, but only in terms of the odd missionary meeting at which a missionary on furlough would speak and be followed by cups of tea and various buttered breads!

Within Ireland itself in those post-Second World War days the church—any church—stood within society as an integral part of it. The concepts of the church, Christian faith and regular worship, the Bible and prayer book that could be found in almost every Church of Ireland home—these were inextricably woven into people's lives at all points, not just at moments of celebration and crisis. As clergy it was presumed that we would conduct public worship to which almost everyone in the Church of Ireland community would come. We would teach the Christian faith to children and adults and visit parishioners in homes, hospitals, nursing homes, and every other place where people lived out their lives. We would be welcome at any time in any school of our own tradition. Concepts such as formal Christian education were still in the future, so teaching adults meant sermons. Rightly or wrongly, it was taken for granted that men and women knew the tenets of the Christian faith, just as it was taken for granted that they were nourished by their mother's milk. It was to take only two generations in the decades since then to prove how illusory this comfortable assumption was!

An incident that occurred in my very first week of ministry expresses much of that long-ago situation. I was doing my first visits, working my way along a terrace of houses on the south side of Dublin Bay. I was excruciatingly new, even to every stitch of clothing that I wore. My bicycle shone, my collar was pristine starched linen, my enthusiasm was at fever pitch. I suspect I thought of myself as a formidable force in the armies of the Lord!

I approached a gleaming suburban front door and pushed the bell. Nothing happened at first. I tried again. I was about to try a third time when the door opened a few inches. A man in his early forties looked around the edge of the door. It was a thin face, heavily mustached, topped with dark tousled hair, and obviously displeased. He looked at me in a long-suffering way. I made the usual bright and cheerful and positive self-introduction, presuming that it would be met by the same cheerful welcome I had hitherto been accorded everywhere else. This time there was a terrible silence, which he broke by saying with a kind of devastating simplicity and bleakness, "I was in my bath."

I was at a loss. Nobody had ever given me instructions for dealing with this kind of frigid encounter. I must have stammered out some kind of apology for making him arise dripping and obviously swearing from the comfort of the tub. Again there was a silence while he received this, still looking at me from sad, rather languid eyes. "Have fun," he then said with chilling economy, and closed the door. I was devastated. Hurt, mystified, embarrassed, feeling a fool, thinking of all the brilliant replies I could have made but didn't, I immediately headed for a house where I knew I would be given a warm welcome.

The following Tuesday I was going through my week's visiting with the rector, and I told him of the encounter. His response was immediate. He told me the man's story, a sad one but typical of that post-war time. A very gifted scientist who had gone to work in a large laboratory in England just before the war, the man returned to the safety of Ireland's neutrality when war came. Some years later, when the war was over, he had tried to be accepted again in the English scientific community but had been rejected. He had settled in Ireland again, extremely embittered and increasingly withdrawn.

I can remember the relief with which I heard this news. As I look back now I am amused by the fact that it allowed me, in a way I did not then realize, to look at this encounter with rejection as the exception that proved the rule. It allowed me to assume that normality would always be in terms of receiving welcome, pleasantness, encountering solidarity in the faith and affirmation of my priesthood. In these assumptions I was typical of that time and place. But time was to prove us wrong in a few short decades.

a time before this

I t is a Friday night, sometime in the winter of 1951. A cold, wet Dublin night, the rain comes down in straight lines. Beginning outside the foyer of the largest movie house in the city is a solid line of people that stretches at least two blocks. Some crouch under umbrellas; others huddle together in a fruitless effort to stay dry and warm. They are waiting to get into a movie. At this time, before television has come to the country, Ireland is crazy about movies. Even a night like this one does not keep the lines from forming.

Suddenly one of the uniformed staff of the movie theater begins to move down the line, flashlight in hand, its beam catching the driven raindrops and emphasizing the appalling night. Every now and then he stops, directs the light on a huddled figure, and says solicitously, "Ah, there y'are, Father. Come on up with me outa the rain." Obediently the good Fathers—because there would never be a single priest in such circumstances—edge out of the surrounding mass of sodden humanity and run, heads down against the rain, until they disappear into the shining warmth of the distant and, as yet for the rest of us, unattainable foyer. This invitation would be repeated all the way down the line whenever a clerical collar was found. No voice would be raised in protest, but as soon as the good Fathers were out of earshot some eloquent comments on the situation could be heard all down the line!

I recall this moment to bring out a point about clergy and society that can very easily be forgotten. I think it is valid to say that most clergy today, particularly when they are beginning their ministry, base whatever confidence they have on the quality of their training in seminary. There is nothing wrong with this source of confidence, but it is something that has come only in relatively recent years. In previous generations, the confidence of clergy beginning their ministry came from the realization that the society they were entering affirmed and accepted their role without question. Certainly this was true in Ireland, and while it may have been at its highest level in the Roman Catholic community, it was true for all Christian traditions in the country. In the 1940s and 1950s, to be a priest in Ireland—in fact to be a cleric of any faith—was regarded not only as quite normal, but even as admirable. In the Roman Catholic Church being a priest was positively awe-inspiring, and all the more remarkable because it could be mingled with the most earthy criticism of a priest's personal behavior and idiosyncracies, criticism that was somehow entirely divorced from a deep reverence for that mysterious thing called his priesthood.

In those earlier decades of this century, nobody was yet muttering even vague references to "the emperor's clothes" worn by the clergy of the church. There were small pockets of anti-clericalism, but they were confined mostly to the artistic community, particularly writers, who were often enraged by the rigorous and uncompromising censorship openly exercised by the church. By and large the role of the ordained person was fully acknowledged as valid, valuable, even essential to the society. It would have been unthinkable to say otherwise.

I mention this point because it helps to explain something that people today find difficult to understand. To offer oneself as a priest in today's society is to face the challenges of increasing secularization and its consequent ambivalence about the church and therefore about the relevance of the priest's role. The tendency today is to marginalize the functions of the priest in society. Priests are expected to live with a much greater degree of criticism today because of contemporary mistrust of the church's institutions and traditions. Our seminary days prepared us for ministry in a world that was very different and far less demanding.

I don't know to what degree it was intentional—the concept of planning was almost unknown in the Church of Ireland in those days—but the church of my seminary days offered its clergy-in-training one particularly rich resource. It recognized with a kind of quiet wisdom that what one learned in lectures and examinations was not really the heart of things. That heart lay rather in exposing the ordinand to as large a variety of mentors as possible. First there would be the mentors he would meet while in college. To make this possible, every figure of the world church who came to Ireland was brought to the college to have some contact with us. Anthony Bloom, then the very young Patriarch of the Russian congregation in Great Britain, was an attractive presence whose addresses gave us contact with a world of Christian spirituality otherwise totally beyond our ken. Bishops from as far away as Africa and the Arctic brought their wisdom and experience to enrich our training. Two voices and faces among these mentors remain particularly vivid for me.

One memory is of Raymond Raines, Prior to the Community of the Resurrection in Mirfield in Yorkshire, who had recently arrived in Dublin. At that time he was a well-known leader in the life of the Church of England, a respected voice in the Anglo-Catholic wing of the church. He was an imposing figure because of his height, his gaunt, finely-boned face, and his long, flowing black cassock and cloak that he wore at all times as the habit of the community.

During his visit to the college, Father Raines spoke to us at the Theological Society. Draped massively and lazily in one of the worn armchairs that grace the rooms of the society, with students spread around on even lesser chairs or on the floor, literally at his feet, he spoke very quietly but firmly, giving his opinion about certain aspects of the church at that time. From his sprawled figure ascended an unending blue pillar of cigarette smoke.

Father Raines was capable of great sarcasm. Telling us of a recent large English ecumenical conference in which the Church of England had participated against his advice, he informed us that at one stage of the proceedings he became so disgusted that it was only by the grace of God that he was prevented from rising and offering a motion that the work of

the whole conference be dedicated to Saint Pande-
monium! This witticism was rounded off with per-
fect timing by the flicking of a long cigarette ash in
the general direction of the nearby fireplace.

Today that cavalier attitude might seem very distant to most Christians. Yet it was Raines who more
than anyone else gave us a vision of the catholicity of
the tradition to which we belonged. Such a degree of
Anglo-Catholicism was not part of the life of the Irish
church for all sorts of reasons, historical and political,
but the knowledge that it existed widened our vision
of the communion in which we were one day to be
clergy.

With equal vividness and gratitude I recall three
evenings spent in the presence of Stephen Neill, then
Bishop of Tinavelly in the Church of South India,
and an extraordinarily articulate speaker. Neill gave
me one of the most formative experiences of my ministry. For three evenings he lectured on the history of
Christian missions. Neill walked into our small island
world and unfurled a map of the whole world, the
real world far beyond our shores. True, we had some
images of it, but they were pitifully limited. A missionary project here, a magazine article about this or
that piece of infinitely distant exotica, a tea organized
for a returned missionary preceded or followed by
an illustrated lecture. Neill changed all that for many
of us, making us realize that there were great Christian communities on every continent.

Looking back, I now realize that Neill—who with
that family name must have had some Irish roots
himself—was reminding us as Irish ordinands that
while we had a long Christian history we needed to

develop a much wider Christian geography. Even further, he was telling us that we needed to develop a geography that went far beyond Christianity, and to face the fact that we shared the planet with other great spiritualities.

Not many years later, one lovely early summer evening in Ontario, I went to a meeting, thinking it was just another of those endless meetings that are part of clergy life. A priest had come from Toronto to address the clergy of the diocese about the relationship between the Canadian province of the Anglican Communion and the other provinces of the communion. His name was Morse Robinson, and he was later to be a bishop in the Canadian church. For a second time my mind was deeply challenged to a vision of the wholeness of the Christian community across the world. I left that evening thrilled and excited beyond measure, realizing as I had done previously with Stephen Neill, that I must never allow my vision of the church to become small and limited.

For me, these two people performed the role of the *curraghs* in early Celtic times. They bore me from an island existence, setting me out on seas where I would become aware of the infinite varieties of Christian communities, Christian worship, and Christian service. In this discovery and in this response to voices that spoke of a greater world, I was, in a very small and humble way, experiencing that motivation that made it impossible for so many Celtic Christians of an earlier time to make the boundaries of their own small island the measure of the Body of Christ.

chapter 19

a morning walk

e arly on the morning of July 12, 1952, I walked up Dame Street in the heart of the city of Dublin, out of the front gate of Trinity College, and eventually entered the gates of Christ Church Cathedral. In doing so I went back in time from the sixteenth century to the tenth. Behind me, visible through the main gate, stood that part of the university built by the first Elizabeth and known to this day as "The Rubrics" because of its red color and brick structure. As I went the length of Dame Street I could from time to time look north along a side street and catch a glimpse of the Liffey, the long slow river that links Dublin Bay with the central plains and pastures of the midlands, the river that turns up again and again in James Joyce's writing as Anna Livia.

The moment I turned into the gate leading to the grounds of the cathedral, I stepped back half a millennium beyond the Elizabethans. Now I was in the world of the Norsemen. Here, bringing their long-boats this far in from the sea—and they were always extremely wary of going too far inland—the Norse built a town on the river bank. On that day in 1952 neither I nor anyone else knew that such a town ever existed. It would lie hidden until the 1970s, when it

would see the light of day again by the chance striking of the blade of a bulldozer excavating for a new
high-rise development.

I could have described this short Sunday morning
walk in other ways, too. As I passed under the front
arch of Trinity College I walked between the statues
of Edmund Burke, orator, statesman, parliamentar-
ian, and Oliver Goldsmith, poet, romantic, and, for
most of his life, pauper. About twenty minutes later,
as my walk would be measured in ordinary time, I
would go along the south aisle of the great cathedral,
passing the recumbent stone effigy of Strongbow,
leader of the Norman knights whose ships docked
on the quayside at Wexford on a cold windy day in
December 1171 and by doing so changed forever the
relationship between Ireland and Britain.

You could measure this walk in terms of its mingling of architectural styles and eras, from the gray
stone walls of Dublin Castle to the graceful Georgian
doorways and windows on every side. Or you could
measure these paces in terms of those men and
women who walked it so often before me in their
own time, not least among them John Henry Cardi-
nal Newman, Jonathan Swift, George Bernard Shaw,
Lady Gregory, William Butler Yeats, and Sean O'Casey.

Why is it second-nature to me to describe an otherwise very ordinary walk in these ways? I could just
as easily have described the city blocks as my eye
and ear encountered them that morning. Why not?
Because there is something about being the child of
an old culture that makes one naturally aware of the
many histories hidden in any given geography, and
these histories—some of them heroic and some

shameful—belong to oneself. All of these things I have mentioned are, in their various ways, what has formed me to this moment in time. They are who I am.

Passing the effigy of Strongbow, I move into the large, dark wood-panelled sacristy of Christ Church Cathedral. It seems to me that there is a maze of rooms and chambers in this part of the building, open and closed, used and unused, cleaned or neglected for years. In one room there are bookcases, some with glass fronts and others with open shelves. Almost every book is leather-bound. Some are the Bibles, prayer books, altar books, and litany manuals of the cathedral's liturgical life over the years. I notice one large volume lying on its side; when I glance at it quickly, I see that it dates from the seventeenth century. The books lie or stand in casual profusion, uncatalogued and, it would seem, largely uncared for. I have been in this room since that time and much has been done to remedy all this clutter, but I have a feeling that up to about the Second World War these things were somehow seen as still the instruments of contemporary life and work. The past was seen not so much as the past as merely an earlier part of the present, undivided and somehow one seamless tapestry of time.

Hearing the distant sound of voices I continue toward the robing room itself. It seems huge. The center of the room is occupied by a vast gleaming table surrounded by high, upright chairs. All around the walls are wardrobes interspersed by bookcases and shelves. Today the place is full of clergy in various stages of ecclesiastical vesting and robing. All of them are men, as would have been usual then, and all are my elders, some considerably so.

Today there are four of us being ordained deacons. There are many hearty handshakes as many voices wish us well. There is some gentle ribbing—"Just wait, young man!" "Oh, you'll learn all about it!" "Still time to change your mind, you know!"—arms on the shoulder at various moments, a slap or two on the back. Without anyone actually saying it, I am receiving the message that I am stepping over some kind of line. I am being received into a fellowship. How often have I done the same as these men during the years since, watching as those to be ordained put on their spotless new robes and prepared to begin their ministry as priests, seeing an earlier version of myself, wishing a young man or woman well, saying a quick silent prayer that they may find fulfillment in their chosen way.

Of the four who are presented for ordination today, three of us are in our early-to-mid-twenties, while the fourth is older, perhaps in his early fifties, married and with grown children. None of us younger men have ever been involved in any other job or profession. We have, for better or for worse, moved through the sequence taken for granted in those days for youth of our tradition—primary school, secondary school, boarding school, university.

Because the morning is bright and dry, the procession of clergy will first move outside, past the ruins of the twelfth-century abbey on this spot, its dark stones half-hidden in the long, unkempt grass. We turn into the west door and re-enter the gray stone world of the cathedral. The congregation is already singing. The rest I barely remember; it is like a dream. At some stage we sing the Irish hymn "Be Thou My Vision," one that will remain beloved to me as long as I live. Nothing of the homily remains in my memory except one sentence. The preacher pointed to the stone step on which we were soon to kneel and said, "Never forget that on the stone where you are to be ordained, priests have been ordained for nine hundred and fifty years."

Then came the moment when we went forward. I knelt down. I had the sense of being surrounded by many people and I felt the pressure of many hands, the placing of a stole around my body. Time passed as in a dream. A small square of bread was placed in my palm, a chalice held for a moment and dark wine tasted. Once again I heard voices, the organ burst into the recessional hymn. We turned down the aisle and emerged from the echoing shadows into the sunlight.

ín pRaíse of otheRs

arthur Hamilton Butler was in his early forties when I went to be his curate. He enjoyed taking newly ordained clergy, keeping them with him for two or three years and forming them from the ground up. The very first day I sat opposite him in his study he made my position quite clear. "There are two things of absolute importance," he said, speaking in the rather clipped peremptory tone he had picked up in his war years as a senior chaplain with the British army. "You must understand that to me and everyone here in the parish you are a young man learning his job. The second thing is that I wish you to be completely loyal to me, and I will do everything I can to help you do your job well." As an introduction it could hardly be clearer or simpler. In fact, in its own way it was very reassuring. One knew exactly where one stood.

I owe Arthur Butler much of whatever I have been able to contribute to the church. He was a strict disciplinarian, which I needed. He was a most careful and sensitive liturgist and an excellent communicator. Pastorally he was utterly realistic about people, understanding, charitable, and compassionate. Because of his war years, where he had shared some of that conflict's most brutal moments in the Anzio beachhead in Italy, there had formed in him a capacity for tolerating the weaknesses of humanity while at the same time being able to challenge people to take hold of their lives and to be responsible for their actions.

Perhaps the most valuable learning I was given by Arthur Butler was the result of his experiences outside the Church of Ireland. For some years he had been on the staff of one of the most well-known communicators in the Church of England at that time. This, coupled with his army experience in Europe, had made him realize that very different worlds of Christian faith, social change, and secularization lay outside Ireland, all of which would one day affect its life.

The result of this awareness was his constant demand for high standards in every aspect of our work in the parish. Slovenliness in anything—worship, preaching, following up pastoral needs—was inexcusable. He felt that the life of the Church of Ireland at that time had become too lax, too comfortable, too out of touch with the tide of ideas flowing around it and now lapping at its shores. In these and many other ways Arthur Butler was a mentor for me in my earliest years of ministry. I also suspect that I looked to him as a father figure in the years immediately following my own father's death. We remained friends for the rest of his life as he became a bishop first in the west of Ireland and later in the crucible of Belfast during its decades of agony that still continue as I write.

The invitation to go to Canada came out of the blue one winter's day after I had been in my first curacy for about a year. It came from John Anderson, rector of a parish in Winnipeg. One of his church wardens was a first cousin of my mother who had emigrated to Canada back in the early 1920s. I did not realize it then, but many young clergy were receiving invitations from both Canada and the United States as parish churches there boomed after the war. To this letter, inviting me to join him in St. Aiden's in Winnipeg, I wrote saying that I could not leave the Church of Ireland for two years because of the financial aid I had been given in my senior years at Trinity College. A year later I heard from John Anderson again, saying that he was now dean of the diocese of Ottawa and inviting me to join the staff of his cathedral there.

Those who cross the Atlantic today with casual frequency cannot imagine how far away and romantic the North American continent was to someone of my generation. To be invited to work there was immensely exciting. Eventually I found myself heading out on my journey, going up the gangway of the *SS Franconia*, an ancient and by then shabby Cunarder that creaked and groaned its way across the northern Atlantic in late October and eventually disgorged me and many others at a Montreal dockside, where we were guided onto trains for our various destinations. As I looked out the window at the early winter countryside sliding by, I could not help recalling a childhood memory. As a small boy, whenever I was disobedient, my mother would say to me, "If you're not good, you'll be sent to your Auntie Sis in Canada!"—a warning that would be communicated with great frowns and threatening looks. She was referring to her eldest sister, who had emigrated many years before and was even now awaiting my arrival in Ottawa within a few hours. I was at last on my way to meet Auntie Sis! The truth is, I could not have been given a warmer welcome and for nearly a year she provided me with the most comfortable home imaginable.

Standing behind her that day on the platform when I arrived was a tall, fine-looking man with a friendly, open, smiling face, a deep and very relaxed voice, and a handshake ready and firm in spite of his considerable wartime injuries. John Anderson, my future boss and second rector, was very different from my former rector. A western Canadian, he was lanky, easygoing, and relaxed. At first I had difficulty accepting his ways of doing things because they were so different from those of my first rector, but I soon found that his relaxed manner did not mean he was neglectful, unfocused, or careless. I think that, more than anything else, he taught me to have a sense of proportion about events and challenges and problems. The greatest gift he had to give me was serenity; he told me once that after he had gone over a mine in a jeep and spent two years in the hospital hanging between life and death, anything else in his life tended to be rather easily managed! After I left him to move to a different place, we remained friends until his death at much too early an age from those same lingering war wounds.

Another mentor, Ernest Reed, was my first bishop in Canada, whose consecration had taken place shortly before I arrived in his diocese. He had a natural authority that communicated itself easily. Because

I was on the staff of the cathedral I saw him frequently. Reed was very much alive mentally, physically, and spiritually. He was immensely energized by the changes that were just beginning to take place as the 1950s drew to a close and the 1960s began. He was interested in the new voices just beginning to sound at the time, voices of people such as John Robinson, who would soon publish *Honest to God*, and Harvey Cox, author of *The Secular City*. He was excited, too, by the growing self-realization of Anglicanism as a world-wide communion of churches. He traveled widely, preached effectively, encouraged and affirmed his clergy. He died instantly one day in a great burst of hearty laughter, his head thrown back as his body slumped to the floor. The vitality of his life and faith still resounds in the lives of many of us who were young in his diocese at that time.

Such was the world of my mentors after ordination, the faces and voices of the communion of saints that each of us has if we only realize it. I know that each of these people would smile at my calling them mentors, but they were mentors to me and because of being in their company I find something happening in my own later years of ministry. I think it was Erik Eriksen who defined the later stage of life as best spent in being what he called generative. I find that it is immensely satisfying to generate some new thought or self-discovery in a younger woman or man now in ordained ministry. Particularly in recent years, the occasions at the College of Preachers in Washington, D.C. when I have seen young priests discover a particular preaching gift they had not realized they possessed have been richly satisfying. Perhaps one such moment will afford a smile and provide an ending to these thoughts about mentors.

I'll call him Peter. We had been working on the effort to preach a homily without referring to the manuscript one had prepared. It was an admittedly terrifying idea to him, but toward the end of the week enough trust had built up for him to try it among his peers. He stood at the lectern, white-knuckled. I could see the sweat on his forehead. But, like the good apostle Peter, this Peter launched out into the deep against his own instincts. A couple of times he nearly sank, but eventually he made it to the end, emotionally exhausted but triumphant.

The conference went on, and the time came for us to scatter homeward. I thought no more about Peter's triumph until about a month later, when I got a postcard that now has a proud place in my scrapbook. All it said was, "Herb—I did it. It worked. They loved it. Peter." Peter had been set free. He had discovered a gift he didn't know he possessed. That is reason for great joy and thanksgiving, to be a mentor to someone as one has also been mentored.

the missionary
box

Once again it is the month of July and once again I am walking from Trinity College to Christ Church Cathedral in Dublin. The year is 1991, thirty-nine summers from my ordination, thirty-nine summers from that walk to the cathedral in 1952. Along this street the vast changes of these four decades are hardly apparent other than in the density of traffic. The buildings remain very much as they were that morning. Certainly the broad stone front of Trinity College is exactly the same. Burke and Goldsmith still stand on their pedestals, while across from them the huge Romanesque front of the Bank of Ireland testifies to the permanence of economic systems. At the far end of the street the cathedral testifies to another kind of permanence, that of the human search for faith and meaning. As I approach it I notice that its grounds are in better shape than I remember. The old Norman ruins have been set off more clearly, and the efforts at restoration inside the cathedral are obvious in the polished stone and stained glass windows.

As in all old world cities, however, appearances are deceptive. North American cities are in some ways more honest with the person who returns, as I have, after some years. Where once a row of houses stood, there may now be a high-rise; where there once was a school, there is a parking garage. In old cities in Europe and the British Isles the row of houses is much more likely to be there still, but it will be merely the appearance that remains—their interiors have become luxury flats or condominiums. Old shop fronts remain, but behind their stone faces there will be a video store, a drugstore, an espresso bar. To some degree this is true in this long Dublin street, but the changes here, because they are still framed in old buildings, have a feeling of continuity with the past. There is a suggestion that the past has not so much been jettisoned as adapted and molded to a present that will itself in time pass away and change into something else.

Huge changes have come to this island where I was born and grew up. Nothing less than the continent of Europe itself is coming here, reaching out into the Atlantic and ending the isolation of this island that Agricola saw to the west as his Roman galley sailed north between Britain and Ireland. It is often said that one of the significant factors in the history of Germany was that the Roman legions never conquered it, and the same applies to Ireland. The sea between Britain and Ireland was to Ireland as Hadrian's Wall was to Scotland. But all such walls and natural barriers are being demolished by the huge trucks, the planes, the television channels, the business contracts, the Eurostock markets, the multi-nationals.

Inside Christ Church Cathedral, just as on the day I was ordained, Strongbow still lies recumbent on his tomb, as he has done for almost a thousand years. If there is any sentiment or nostalgia in the things I have said, he would have scant patience with me. After all, Strongbow himself and his knights came from Europe, from the coasts of Normandy to the hills of Wales. After they consolidated their power so much that they felt the English king to be threatened by them, they decided to go further. One day they thundered down the ramps of their ships in Wexford Harbor at almost exactly the same spot as the ferries today disgorge the endless trucks.

So today I take Strongbow as my companion, sitting once again in a pew near his tomb, aware of the time that has passed since I came here to be ordained. Had I but known it, that walk to the cathedral on my ordination day was leading me and everyone else of that generation toward a time of unimaginable change, and yet something even now gives me pause. Perhaps those who trained us were wiser than we thought. As I look back I realize how little those who provided our training concerned themselves with the world of our own time. Their chief concern was that the tradition passed on to them be passed on to us, and because of that they spoke to us more of the past than of the present. So we became aware of the succession of past faithfulness, of the apostles, of the early Christian communities in the cities of the Roman Empire, of the early church fathers, the great controversies and heresies of which contemporary spirituality contains so many variations. We became aware of those whom we were taught to call saints, especially those of our own and the neighboring islands. We learned too of the giants of Christian thought through those past centuries.

The effect of all this emphasis on the ideas and people who had gone before us was to hand on to us a sense of a very long story, not so much past as timeless. During the years of my formation I was being told that there had been periods of great change and challenge long before my lifetime and there would be such times long after I had lived—although I must confess that nobody told there would be a period of apocalyptic change *within* my lifetime!

For many years I had a little wooden log cabin about six inches long by four inches wide, and about four inches high. On the ridge of the roof was a chimney stack and set into the roof was a narrow slit for a child to put coins in. Covering the brown wood of the roof was a large label identifying the box as the property of the Commonwealth and Continental Church Missionary Society.

I was given this box as a child by the missionary who came to speak to us in our parish school. In it I put pennies from time to time—pennies which, along with many others, went to the work of the church in faraway western Canada. I had seen magic lantern slides of western Canada and was full of highly romanticized dreams about it. My dreams were particularly encouraged by a line drawing on the label across the roof of my missionary box which showed a clearing in a Canadian forest. Across the clearing a dog team was pulling someone on a sled.

Above the trees, in the clear endless sky, was a small, single-engine plane. These images were the stuff of infinite romance to me, and even though the missionary box has long since disappeared, they have always remained in my mind.

I was using that box in 1940—I remember the date because I know it was before I went away to boarding school. Eventually I went away to school and time rolled on, from school to university, from university to first parish, on to Canada, parishes, marriage, children, and suddenly it was 1988. I was sixty years old, an experienced rector of a number of parishes, staying in the city of Regina, Saskatchewan to lead a clergy conference. The conference had gone well and the bishop, an old friend of mine, drove me to the airport for a late afternoon flight home to Calgary. It was a glorious evening in late springtime and the prairie landscape was breathtakingly beautiful, the light brilliant, the sky stretching away forever.

The bishop dropped me at the airport but when I went in I found that my flight had been postponed for an hour and a half, so I decided to check my bag and go for a walk. This airport is not huge, so it was easy to walk away from it and into a nearby area of grass. I shared the grass with two large rabbits who sat in the long grass, gazing at me watchfully.

I was about half a mile to the east of the airport when I heard the sound of an engine revving up. I looked back toward the airport building, but at first I couldn't see anything because the sun lowering toward the west was in my eyes. But the sound of the engine grew even stronger and I looked again. Then I saw a small, single-engine plane rise above the building, exactly like the little plane on my long-lost missionary box. Flying now in the sky above the real western Canada, it crossed my sight from left to right, flying north. Very quickly it became a speck in the sky and then disappeared, the sound of its engine dying away into silence.

I am not sure how to express the feelings of that moment. Amazed delight, perhaps, and the immediate realization of an epiphany, a moment that is more than itself, when something unsought is given, something unlooked for is made visible. I think above all that something happened to time within me. In some way my life had just been bracketed. Past time and present time became one, my early years and later years linked and the whole given a kind of unity.

I remember no sense of sadness, no regretting that so much of life has been lived, no wishing that I could go back to being the boy who once held the missionary box and looked not so much at it as into it, deeply. Rather, the feeling was of gratitude for a gift received. If I were to try to define what the gift was—and I am wary of trying to define moments of epiphany—I think I would say that two very different stages of my life were knit together without any effort on my part. For a fleeting moment I had a sense of being whole, of *shalom*.

the leap
of the deer

a mid the general clutter of my study is a small cross about a foot high, a framed and inscribed text of the hymn "Saint Patrick's Breastplate," an old print of a ninth-century round tower, and a scripted version of the old Irish hymn "Be Thou My Vision." For some years now the church has seen a renewed fascination with a phenomenon thought of as Celtic spirituality, based on Celtic Christianity. Celtic lore was almost unheard of until recently, and yet now it is becoming common currency. Perhaps these items now in my study but rooted in my Irish past can provide a few clues as to the reasons for this sudden interest.

When I was in school we had to study an essay of John Henry Newman's called "The Isles of the North." In it Newman tells of the shadow of barbarian invasions engulfing western Europe in the fifth century and the consequent movement of Christian communities and institutions to what was then the edge of the world—the coasts of Britain and Scotland and the interior of Ireland. Here, in a climate and culture very different from that of the Mediterranean world, the flame of Christian life began to burn warmly and brightly. For five hundred years, from the fifth century through the ninth, we meet saints of the Christian faith who have become part of the heritage of the whole church. We see developing a monastic movement of immense enthusiasm, discipline, learning, and art, which then explodes into mission. It spills out beyond Ireland, first into Iona and from there into the lowlands of Scotland and the north of England, and from there it eventually crosses the North Sea, penetrates Europe along the great rivers of France and Germany, and even finds its way down the Danube to link up with eastern church life. On the way we encounter such names as Patrick, Columba, Ninian, Brigid, Gall, Columbanus, and Hilda of Whitby.

To include this essay of Newman's in the school curriculum of Irish children was no casual choice. Its message was quite clear: in earlier centuries Irish Christianity made a major contribution at a most difficult time in Christian history, a claim that I think is justified by the evidence. But I suspect that there is another aspect to this flowering of faith on the edge of the world that may speak to western Christians in the late twentieth century, who are experiencing the marginalization of Christian faith in recent decades in the west, the pushing of Christian faith not so much to the geographical as to the cultural margins of western society. In recent years there has been ample evidence to suggest that Christian faith is refusing to stay in exile on those margins and is in many ways showing signs of making its way back toward the center of contemporary life. In this sense it may

be that the contemporary church, consciously or un-
consciously, sees its life as sharing the experience of
the Celts between the fifth and ninth centuries.

Consider the black, twelve-inch-high cross on my
window sill. It is a replica of one of the finest stone
crosses still standing in Ireland, the Cross at Monasterboice in County Louth. My memory tells me that
the original is about eight or nine feet high. As far as
anyone knows, the first Norse attack on an Irish
monastery was made in 795 on Rathlin Island off the
coast of Antrim. These attacks were to continue for
over a century. At first it was obvious that the main
objective was robbery—gold and silver ornaments, as
well as vessels of the sanctuary, crosses, chalices,
bells, and illuminated manuscripts, would all be
taken. Later this pattern changed to more frequent
murders of monks and nuns, while later still the
Norsemen began the practice of taking hostages. A
monk or nun would be ransomed for a certain sum,
an abbot or a bishop or a local chieftain for a great
deal more. It was in the face of these raids that sometime around the middle of the ninth century the Irish
retreated from working solely in wood and metal
and began to work in stone. Since these stone monu-
ments had no intrinsic value and could be moved
only with great difficulty, the great stone crosses began to appear all over the country.

When I look at my replica of one of these ancient
crosses, in my mind I often find myself standing in a
field under a gray, moving sky. It could be that the
sea is within sight, but it could also be a small, dark
lake with the foam of what we called "white horses"
on its surface and low blue hills beyond. Different

landscapes appear to the inner eye because these crosses were built in many places, sometimes near a monastery, sometimes in a place of burial where in later centuries there would be a shrine or a place of pilgrimage.

As I lift this small cross, I remember how every square inch of the original is covered in carving. Every area of carving is a scene from the Bible, particularly the life of Christ. Each scene is set in a panel about a foot square. On a recent visit to the National Museum in Dublin I was looking at a large illustration of this particular cross at Monasterboice. It occurred to me suddenly that I was looking at a bank of video screens, a thought all the more striking because I know these crosses were used for teaching the gospel to an illiterate population in those early centuries. After all the centuries in between, we have once again returned to a world in which communication is primarily by images. It is not too wildly imaginative to think that a priest of the ninth century would not take long to identify with my home video screen.

Then consider the words to a lovely old Irish hymn, a favorite of mine. The first line is "Be thou my vision, O Lord of my heart." As you read or sing it as a late twentieth-century person, you cannot but notice how it addresses God not with abstractions, but in a rich succession of images strung together like a lovely necklace. In rapid succession God is named as my vision, my light, my wisdom, my high tower, my sword, my true word, my father, my indwelling, my high king, heaven's sun, heart of my heart, my ruler.

In these images it is fascinating to see a way of communicating that is very typical of Celtic culture and spirituality. There is little sustained teaching. I think I am correct in saying that no great tradition of sustained systematic theology has come from those times—if there is, I have no memory of it being mentioned to me as something to be proud of! The Celts were much more inclined to communicate their passionate faith in images, the images of the illuminated Gospel page, the image carved in stone on the cross, the quick verbal image in poetry or song. The image is offered to the listener or to the eye to be received and worked on by the imagination and the emotions. Notice in this hymn the mixture of images. There is the inner world—my light, my wisdom, heart of my heart—but there is also the utter realism of the outer world and its harsh struggle, for this God is my sword for the fight, my high tower. It seems to me that the primary gift of those times in Ireland was the telling of stories, the recitation of poems, sagas, and runes, the passing on of myths, the composing of hymns.

Finally, consider the hymn called "Saint Patrick's Breastplate," a scripted version of which I have framed on my wall. I remember a few years ago becoming aware particularly of its fourth verse:

> I bind unto myself today
>> The virtues of the starlit heavens,
>> The glorious sun's lifegiving ray,
>> The whiteness of the moon at even,
>> The flashing of the lightning free,
>> The whirling wind's tempestuous shocks,

> The stable earth, the deep salt sea
> Around the old eternal rocks.

This verse stands out from the rest of the hymn, which is far more traditional theologically. It is almost as if the unknown poet—writing, it is generally thought, in the ninth century—wanted to express something extremely precious to him that was not in the accepted mainstream of Christian thought. As we read these lines today, we recognize the wish to link Christian faith with the surrounding created order. We are hearing an expression of something that we are once again desperately trying to express in our own time, a revitalized Christian theology of the natural environment. I cannot help wondering if this link with creation is among the reasons for our renewed interest in these Celtic centuries.

Ironically, anyone who has grown up in a place heavy with history, as I did, tends to take it very much for granted, especially (and for obvious reasons) in childhood. Even in later life we can live in places that are incalculably rich in history and be not in the least interested or concerned. I have seen children playing on a Jerusalem hillside that holds within it at least four millennia of biblical history. When I myself was a child in Cork, during the short time we lived on the south side of the city I had to go to school every day through streets that at one point passed under an arch that dated from the eleventh or twelfth century. It was not of the slightest interest to me, not because I didn't care, but for a reason difficult to put into words. I knew how old the arch was because I had been told in school, but the arch also belonged to me in the sense that it was part of me and of my story. In that sense, and in that sense only, did I take it for granted.

It is the same with everything else I have written about in these pages. When I lived among them they were mine by right of being born among them—the cathedrals, the crosses, the manuscripts, the ruins, the castles, the sacred wells, the roadside shrines, the stories, the songs, the crumbling walls of the Norse, the Norman, and the Elizabethan, the weathered altars of pagan faith that lie half-hidden in fields from a time long before recorded history. The wonder is that they now speak again to many who seem to have need of them and to draw grace from them for living in our troubled and changing time.